THE NEVER FORGOTTEN CHILD

THE STORY OF OUR TEACHER, MARGARET ANNE SAVAGE

JAN PRICE

D1568782

Copyright © 2020 by Jan Price

All rights reserved.

Available on Amazon.com and other retail outlets

STACKS OF BOOKS, INC.

P.O. BOX 308

CLIFTON, VIRGINIA 20124

WWW.STACKSOFBOOKSLIFE.COM

STACKSOFBOOKSLIFE@OUTLOOK.COM

ISBN: 978-1-7320994-2-5

To all the kind people who helped
make me who I am today
And especially my grandparents
who I called Papa and Mama,
And to my mother who I called Mother
and was known as Dolly,
And to my cousin Bob White and my half-brother JK,
To Jill, one of the kindest people I have ever known,
And certainly to Jan Price because without her,
This book would never have been written.
Margaret Savage

———

To Kalli who writes the most beautiful stories
and inspires me to see stories all around
and to write them, too.
Jan Price

CONTENTS

1. You Can Call Me Margaret   1

2. That Little Mind Churning   5

3. Catch A Mischievous Moment   28

4. I Just Loved Teaching   57

5. A Lorelei Calling   82

6. A Pen Is About Perspective   95

7. Still Not Tied To A Mast   101

YOU CAN CALL ME MARGARET

T he year, 1969, we entered Miss Savage's sixth grade class in the small town of Fairfax, Virginia, twenty miles outside of Washington, D.C. To gain perspective, free speech protests took place on the college campus in Berkeley, California in 1964. The riots in Washington, D.C. following the assassination of Martin Luther King, Jr. took place in 1968 and the following year, 1969, Neil Armstrong and Buzz Aldrin bounced about on the moon's surface. In the decade of the 1960's, Hot Wheels and Barbie were in, the Peace Corp began, and Willie Nelson recorded his first album.

We were eleven and twelve years old in 1969 having lived those years within the secure bounds of an elementary school that stood students outside the classroom door for talking too much and possibly bent over in fear of a paddle to the bottom in the principal's office. I did experience the former only once because that was all it took. I never knew what precipitated the latter though my recollection was that Miss Savage kept her class in order with none of that. The school overall left long memories of living and learning and in Miss Savage's class, much more.

Layton Hall Elementary School opened in 1956. Miss Savage began there in 1957, the year some of us were born. I always thought the school was named after a famous person named Layton Hall but after searching now fifty-some years later, the name seems to be of the area in our town known as Layton Hall. Or who was that guy?

The building, of course, was 1950's style, flat-roofed and two stories with two long rows of tall classroom windows running across the front and across the back against austere dark red brick. Those classrooms had all windows on one side and all closets on the other side, tall and wide folding doors, plenty of storage and lots of classroom to spare. Long, straight, looming and enchanting hallways ran down the middle of each of the two floors. Because we were little, they seemed big. I would never forget the details of that wonderful place or the teachers I had there. It felt like a happy place, and a safe place.

At the time, while we were too little to be big kids participating in the unrest, Miss Savage was thirty-four and may have been too old. We were a peaceful bunch. Miss Savage was my favorite teacher of all time. I always knew, too, she was everybody else's favorite teacher.

When people of our age see each other and start talking about Miss Savage being their favorite teacher, when students still remain in touch with her, still think of her, still thank her, I ask why. She would say because she loved teaching. But even the students who did not have Miss Savage wish they had Miss Savage. There are people walking around who had her and are thankful and people walking around who did not have her and still wish they had. They did love the sixth grade teacher they had, I am sure, because that's the kind of school it was.

When I first began thinking about writing about Miss Savage, I stopped by Teddy's house thinking he had been in her class. His older sister, Florence, had. Teddy was, but then got moved out due to overcrowding. He didn't like it then and doesn't like it thinking about it now. Teddy was moved to Mrs. Johnson's sixth grade class which turned out wonderfully, along with the ability to look out of the front of the building at the goings on. Teddy would want to have had both teachers.

Miss Savage lives in Fairfax County still. She lives at the beach in Florida during the winter and the beach in Maryland during the summer, and she deserves this. I think she's in the same shape as when we were in her class, with the same sense of humor and wit but surely the richer by now, pedaling circles every morning on that stationary bicycle as she sees fit. She is still fit. I told her I wanted to write about her, and she said, "Yes." So, we wrote about her together.

When our endeavor began, Miss Savage was preparing to go to Florida for the winter. We maintained contact about life in the coastal sunshine and once she returned in the spring, began pulling together memories of her life. As a writer thinking about all the stories Miss Savage began sending me, I knew it would be full of charm.

As a retired reading teacher knowing how much effort goes into learning to read, I grew over the years to expect adult readers to put their minds to the reading. "Lazy readers" are not for me. The story must come to the reader and the reader must also come to the story. This writing includes all of Miss Savage's stories she shared with me starting from childhood, often in her own words, including her antics and insights. It includes what life was like as a student for her growing up and for us in our elementary school in the neighborhood where she taught. Come prepared to participate as our reader.

Miss Savage told me early on that my writing was lovely and truth be told, her compliment made more than my day. She wrote, "You know, Jan, you can call me Margaret— honest people have called me worse. As a matter of fact, when I met my half-brother for the first time when he was six and I was seventeen, he asked if he should call me 'Half-Margaret Anne.' I told him to call me whatever he wanted."

I wrote back, "Your writing is lovely, too, Margaret Anne! You said to call you Margaret, and I'm taking the liberty just this once to call you 'Margaret Anne.' I can hear your family speaking to their young girl and such a perfect name, I had to try it out."

As the writing went along, we settled on them all, Margaret Anne, Margaret, Miss Savage, and Moggy from way back before "Half-Margaret Anne" came to be. And so the story begins with a question. Why would we never forget Margaret Anne Savage? This is an effort to find out.

THAT LITTLE MIND CHURNING

Margaret Anne Savage was born January 10, 1935. Being quite ill at the time, her mother, Dolly, remained in the hospital, so Margaret Anne went home with her grandparents, her mother's parents. What would have happened had her father been faithful to her mother, had her mother remained with her father? He was not, so she did not. Margaret's life began in the huge, old farmhouse of her grandparents on a big farm on the Eastern Shore of Virginia, surrounded by water on three sides- a channel, a creek, and the Chesapeake Bay.

With all the memories of growing up on the farm, memories of the farmhouse are as meaningful. The front of their farmhouse included a deep front porch and two protruding chimneys, one on each side. Both upstairs and down had hallways, four bedrooms up and one downstairs. Wooden pegs rather than nails held up the floors of the living room, downstairs hallway and bedroom, the oldest part of the house. The back of the house was as large as if it were a separate house, but attached, and not as old. Big, white dormer window style farmhouses back then had parts added on and taken off.

When Dolly and her sister, Mamie, later sold the house to a local doctor, he moved the older front part of the house to town creating his home called "Wainhouse." The back part remained as a guest house.

Annie Rebecca, Margaret's grandmother known to her as Mama, was part American Indian, a no-nonsense sort of person who preferred to be alone. Annie Rebecca was quite smart and played the piano but would play for no one. When Margaret came home from school in the afternoons and heard Mama playing, she would sit outside the farmhouse to listen.

Mama had been previously married to the love of her life who had died. She then married John Revell Kilmon, not to be confused with the Killmons with two l's. John Revell and Annie had a son who died and two daughters, Dolly, Margaret's mother, and Mamie. Dolly's given name at birth was Lily after her aunt. Since she grew not to like the aunt or the name, she later changed her name to "Dolly" who everyone knew her as. Mamie was the favored child Dolly absolutely adored. John Revell Kilmon was known as "Rev" and to Margaret as Papa. Rev was a farmer and fisherman and a fun-loving practical joker who spent all his time entertaining people with his stories and just being fun. Both grandparents were the kindest of people.

When Margaret was a small person and wanted to build things, Mama would keep her busy with a paint brush and bucket of water "painting the fence" or give Margaret a hammer and nails, saw and board, asking her to build Mama something such as a bird house. That endeavor would take all day, Margaret being determined to make the bird house Mama wanted. And what would Mama always say at the end of the day? Mama always told her little Margaret Anne that it was wonderful, that she loved it, and they must put it somewhere.

Never was the message relayed that anything Margaret accomplished was wrong. When learning to do jigsaw puzzles, Mama would tell her, "How very nice," followed with a bet that they could actually make a pretty picture from those pieces. In later years while teaching, Margaret used her grandmother's approach, understanding that never feeling a failure was too important to ignore. She understood and allowed the spirit, the child within her students, to flourish just as hers flourished in her own childhood.

At night in the farmhouse without electricity at that time, Mama and Papa and Margaret would play cards, Old Maid being the game of choice. Papa always stuck the Old Maid card up high so they would choose that one, but she and Mama were much too smart. Then he would try to move the deck around to force them to pick the Old Maid but again, they were much too clever, so they had their own laugh on Papa.

When they played Bingo, Mama was the caller and since Papa could not read, he had trouble with the higher numbers so Margaret was always the winner. It was important for children to feel good about themselves, she learned, and carried that into her teaching. To this day, she does not play the game of Bingo because people get angry when they don't win, and Margaret to this day does not like anger.

Though Papa could not read, he sat with the newspaper in front of him and sure seemed to enjoy it. Margaret never knew if her grandfather wanted her to think he could read or if he was trying to make sense of it. Papa always kept one step ahead whether he could read or not.

Margaret caught on to her Papa's sense of devilment and great fondness for teasing in his kind and loving way. Loving people as he did, Margaret's grandfather went to parties. Once after coming home from a party a couple of miles down the road, he announced that "Sam" was coming for dinner. Who could Sam have been? He explained to his wife, Annie, that Sam was Sam Rayburn, the Speaker of the House meaning the House of Representatives from Washington, D.C., of course.

Rev would never have wandered far enough away from home to have been to a party in Washington, D.C. Sam had come down to the Eastern Shore to the neighbor's party. Annie replied to her husband that Sam was "not the speaker of this house" and to call and tell him not to come. Rev actually did call and cancel the dinner because clearly, part-Native American Annie was "the speaker" of their territory and for Margaret, a happy territory it was.

A party meant more than Papa being the social one. In their house, living with Papa and Mama meant having a party line. At that time, few people had phones and their phone lines were shared, this time among five lucky houses, thus called "a party line," no relation to having a party. That meant when the phone line was used by another "party" in another house, Papa would rush over and listen to their conversation from his line. Papa would begin to meow or bark and the people talking on the phone to each other, not knowing Papa was listening, would start asking each other when they had gotten a cat or dog. And that was only one of his creative party-line maneuvers. Mama would get annoyed, but the fun-loving devilment went on.

MARGARET DID NOT LIVE WITH HER PARENTS, DOLLY AND Jim, before the divorce or after. She always lived with her grandparents, visiting her parents in town a couple of days at a time until they divorced when she was six. Martha watched Margaret while there. She was five years older and the smartest, most beautiful person, Margaret's true best friend.

Once the two got caught building a small fire to heat water for tea and both ended up with a spanking from Dolly. That was an irritating memory never forgotten like Martha would never be forgotten. She learned from Martha who was black that "black is beautiful" and suffered the loss of this wise friend when her parents divorced.

Margaret's mother she called "Mother" was always a part of her life and now, her many memories. Dolly was loved by everyone. After divorcing Jim Savage, Dolly stayed with the Wilson's in the nearby town of Exmore. They, like so many people on the Eastern Shore, were kind. There were very few Jewish families in town and Dolly got a job working for one of the families, the Flaxes. They were not only kind to Dolly, but they were kind to Margaret giving her lots of nice clothes their daughter had outgrown, and toys. The Flaxes sort of saved their lives by their generosity until they moved away when Margaret reached high school. The store was but three miles from the elementary school. When Margaret was school age and became sick, Mr. Flax would lend Dolly his car to get Margaret from the school clinic and take her all the way to Mama and Papa's.

Once Mama had gone away to visit a friend leaving Papa and Margaret to take care of things. They tried to cook and made a mess of things and missed Mama so. They tried making coffee with just boiling water and coffee grounds floating around in it which was awful. It was always high time for Mama to come home!

When Papa was in charge, Margaret exercised a few too many choices. Before going to pick up her mother at the Flax's store one Saturday evening, Margaret was allowed to choose a cowboy outfit to wear. She arrived at the store with cap pistols blazing. Dolly was so embarrassed, but Mr. Flax got behind the counter to "shoot back" and so did some of the clerks which egged Margaret on. Many of the customers standing there chuckled. Both the Flaxes and their store remain a vividly happy childhood memory.

On the farm were other special and important people who influenced Margaret's life. Many worked in the fields raising various vegetables including Irish potatoes known to the young as "arsh patatas." Papa referred to those working there as "my hands." Papa was very close and kind to them and appreciated their work. Margaret appreciated acquiring their children as playmates. Running through the fields, they would put dirt under their top lip to imitate dipping a tobacco powder called snuff, like the grown-ups did.

Tom was Papa's right-hand man and dear to Margaret who always brought him a glass of water to drink while he was working in the fields. She insisted each time that Tom keep the glass. While visiting his wife, Nealie, after Tom passed away, Nealie offered to give all of Mama's drinking glasses back. Margaret declined. They were a gift given in earnest and would remain so.

There was plenty for Margaret to do on the farm during the day with chickens and ducks, pigs and cows, horses and a mule, and most of all, sheep. Growing up on the farm, memories of animals always surface, even memories about birds. Since Margaret loved birds, Mama would sometimes give her a shaker of salt and tell her if she could sprinkle it on a bird's tail, it would become her pet. Many days were spent running trying to get close enough to birds with the salt shaker.

Every time little Margaret Anne found a dead bird, she would tell Mama they had to have a funeral. They would take the dead bird to the flower garden, dig a hole, Mama would say a few words and sing. People did have music at their pet funerals, Margaret was recently reminded watching the British comedy, The Durrells in Corfu, where they sang at a funeral for a dead bat.

Mama got called upon by little Moggy for so many bird funerals, they had more little twig crosses in the garden than flowers. Moggy was known for dropping her lower lip and never more than when finding a dead bird and burying that little creature in the flower garden. The flower garden was full of rose bushes and chrysanthemums which came back every year, and flowers from the seed sales once Margaret got into school fundraising.

Mama ended up buying most of the flower seeds because of the school's promise of nice gifts at the pep talk in the school auditorium. Those fund raisers must go way back to the early 1940's, at least. That lip dropped well before then and well after, even to this day when all is not well. Her mother always talked to her about curling her lip down so low that she might step on it, and about keeping her shoulders back.

Little Moggy grew to believe from Mother that her shoulders were bound to "get there" before the rest of her body, reminding her to hold her shoulders up and be proud. If her shoulders got there before her head did, how would she be able to handle things? Dolly left a few good, lasting impressions to this day. But nothing was more memorable than the farm animals.

The neatest of animals had to be the sheep, thirty in all. Once there was a lamb whose mother died and Papa brought the baby to Margaret who named it "Baby Lamb," not too original. Baby Lamb drank from a bottle and nipple concoction she and Mama had fixed and Baby Lamb followed Margaret everywhere. That lamb would even get into the car leaving this little girl smelling of lanolin. Margaret did not need a dog. She had a sheep!

HAVING LIVE ANIMALS IN HER LIFE, MARGARET KNEW AT AN early age that dolls were for other people. She never liked dolls. Margaret had an aunt in New Jersey who sent her a doll for Christmas. It was a white doll but turned upside down, it was a black doll. Being a small girl, she did not understand this upside-down concept and was a bit afraid of the doll. She knew the anatomy did not work, two heads on one doll. The poor thing needed a bottom half. Still, this was a doll Margaret has to this day and still does not like it.

Another attempt at giving Margaret a doll occurred when she was eight. She found nail polish and painted both the fingernails and the cheeks such a bright red, the doll looked like she had just run out of a whore house in absolute fright. Perhaps coming from a teacher, a more polite name would be, out of a bordello. The truth was, dolls could not play or respond as sheep did, or as well as cats and dogs and horses. Even chickens were more responsive than dolls so no dolls for Margaret.

She did have a foot-and-a-half tall golden teddy bear with eyes that she pulled out and ate, or that is her recollection. This did not seem to cause any complications for Margaret or "My Bear," the only name the bear ever had until deteriorating and being relegated to the trash bin. If bears have souls, this good little bear went to heaven.

Along with dolls, Margaret also did not like chocolate Easter bunnies. Though she loved getting that Easter basket each year, the tall chocolate bunny in the center became suspect. This may have been when she truly learned that things are not always as they seem. She would go to church on Easter Sunday morning and come back to her big, chocolate bunny slumped over and half-melted. Air conditioning, the box kind in windows, or central air conditioning, had not come along yet so the heat was hard on the chocolate bunnies, and revealing. Not only were those bunnies not solid, they also often tasted like perfume. Though Margaret never gave up chocolate, she did give up chocolate Easter bunnies as they gave false impressions which from early on, she was attuned to. Neither dolls nor hollow chocolate bunnies needed to provide companionship anyhow. The Eastern Shore was also rich with interesting people.

Exmore, a quiet hometown with not a whole lot going on, was where Mama shopped for groceries each Saturday. Papa would drive them and go off chatting with everybody. Mama and Margaret would then be waiting in the car, Mama making up fun stories about all the people passing by even though she didn't know them at the time. As it turned out, they led interesting lives.

Margaret later befriended a lady named Monnie Barcroft who cleaned the movie theater and Margaret hated the fact that kids made fun of her for it. One day years later, Monnie came looking for Margaret at the little restaurant that Margaret and her Aunt Mamie ran at Silver Beach to borrow money to buy a car. Dolly commented after, "She is going to a pig's house looking for silk."

Margaret did not have a cent to her name and hated having to turn Monnie down. She later took Monnie to a dress shop to buy her a nice dress, but Monnie wanted to go to the five and dime store where she found a dress. She then asked Margaret to buy bird seed for her pet bird, Petey. Wanting to share everything with everyone made Margaret happy. Winning the lottery and buying a Maserati might make her as happy, but probably not.

Exmore had a bakery run by a lady named Lola. Lola was friends with Dolly and made the most lovely donuts in this very tiny shop, so Margaret thought. They were, in fact, made at The Corner Bakery in a town called Onancock twenty-two miles north. These cream-filled donuts were only five cents each, now eight dollars a dozen and still there today. Finding some way to get to The Corner Bakery in Onancock, Eastern Shore of Virginia comes highly recommended.

On the way from Exmore to Onancock is a town named Keller known for the amazing, yes, Keller Fair. This fair was the most exciting thing that happened on The Shore each year with a huge grandstand, shows and horse racing. The worst year in memory for Margaret was when there was a polio epidemic and not only was going to the fair called off, going anywhere was. Mama and Papa successfully kept Margaret from getting anything that came around, except the measles. What made matters worse, they thought reading would hurt her eyes while having the measles so she was not allowed to read until she recovered. Adventures inside books have always kept Margaret going.

The best year at the Keller Fair was when Monnie Barcroft set a tent on fire. Monnie saw her husband go into the tent where the ladies did a burlesque show so she gathered up pine shatters and set the tent on fire. Monnie, and particularly picturing what she did at the "hot show" that year at the Keller Fair, would not be forgotten. So many people and so many stories from the Eastern Shore would not be forgotten.

MANY PEOPLE NOT FROM THE EASTERN SHORE CAME TO THE Eastern Shore. They were known to the Eastern Shoremen as "Come Here's." They were the most valued of friends, shaping the lives of their neighbors, sharing thoughts and prayers, and food. The farmland was flat, surrounded by beaches, rich in produce and all things from the water having both the Atlantic Ocean and the Chesapeake Bay to draw from. Sanie and Nick Kellam were an old Eastern Shore family on one side and the Marrons from New York on the other side at the point. Captain Marron was in the Navy so the Marrons were often gone.

Everyone wanted to swim at Marron's Point with its ten-or-twelve foot dive into the water. Swimmers had to drive through Papa's farm to get there. Mama and Papa were the watch dogs preventing them. When Papa wasn't home, Margaret had other ideas. She set up a small business starting with buried planks along the road with nails sitting up. She stopped the cars and charged twenty-five cents to access the point. If they paid, Margaret would explain how to avoid the planks going to the right rather than to the left. If they did not pay, bang went their tires. Then, she would charge thirty-five cents to rent a jack to fix the tires. Papa found out about this and put an end to the business though Margaret knew it was darn smart.

Another family from Sweden, two brothers and one sister in their sixties to seventies, lived near enough for Margaret to ride her bike to their house. Their whole house was wallpapered with magazine pages causing Margaret's eyes to wander all over the place. She approached Mama about wallpapering their house with magazines but Mama would have none of it.

Fred Miller, a neighbor from New York with a wonderful accent, had the same birthday as Margaret so he always came to her birthday party. Mama, Papa, Margaret, and Fred ate cake and ice cream and Fred's gift was always five dollars, until he got married. Then Fred Miller eliminated the five dollars which taught Margaret never to marry due to the risk of becoming a miser.

The Moores were neighbors from New York, too, and Mrs. Moore was pregnant and scared and Mama was there for her all the time. Though Mama didn't like people much, she loved her interesting neighbors. Those who came from other places became the dearest of friends, making Margaret's life enriched with cherished memories of generosity, making her a better person. When she taught, she wanted her students, too, to respect others and learn from them because only good can come from that.

The most horrible night was when the Wilner's son died. They were an older couple from England. Mrs. Wilner had played the violin with the London Symphony. Mr. Wilner was a stained-glass artist and shared his sketches and the processes to create beautiful church windows. Dolly was visiting Mama and Papa one night when the phone rang and it was the war department asking to get a message to the Wilners. Their son had been killed in action. Papa would not go. Dolly took Margaret to their house to tell them their only son, a wonderful person, had been killed at war. Margaret began visiting them at least once a week and remained their dear friends. That night has remained with Margaret all her life.

Mama's brother they called "Ducca" came to live with them and helped in the fields. He had snow white hair, was very tan, and clever just like Margaret had snow white hair, was very tan, and clever. They got along magnificently. He drew pictures for her and taught her to draw.

Margaret was six at the time and starting school so Ducca would meet her on rainy afternoons with the horse and cart, being able to handle a horse but not a car. He loved speaking to "people" along the way home as Margaret sat underneath the tarp he had put in place to keep the rain away. Each time, she would jump up to see who he was speaking to and he would push her head back down because the truth was, Ducca was an entertaining fellow and the people he was speaking to were not really there. Margaret returned to a happy home each day on a farm with a lot of land, to a happy family with very little money.

NEXT TO THE FARM WAS A BEACH AREA WITH TWENTY-FIVE cottages. Sanie and Nick owned the land and later when they passed away, it was sold to the families who had built cottages there. Sanie and Nick ran a little beach concession nearby and made ice cream on Sundays. Mama let Margaret ride her bike over for ice cream each Sunday. Sanie and Nick were like another set of parents. Nick was cantankerous to some, but not towards little Moggy. Their grandson, Ronnie, would visit providing Margaret a good friend though "bad" children don't always make good friends. He would come over and break all of the toys and have to go home. "My grandmother said I could stay an hour," he would announce.

Twenty minutes later, Mama would say, "Ronnie, your hour is up!" Off he would go only to return for another round and on it would go.

Margaret's mother, Dolly, and Ronnie's mother, Madge, were best friends and remained so all their lives just as Margaret and Ronnie remained friends all his life. Once their mothers took them to Salisbury, a larger town just north in Maryland, to a store with an elevator and the two got into a fight in the elevator, so their mothers got off and left them on the elevator to fight it out. What a sight for anyone else getting on the elevator.

Margaret would visit her parents who lived in the nearby

town of Belle Haven. Once, her mother was making biscuits handing Margaret dough to knead. "You let her have her dirty little hands in the dough?" her father yelled. They started arguing.

They argued and they argued and then, they divorced. At such a young age, Margaret felt at fault for the divorce and kept this heavy load to herself. Feeling to blame, Margaret came to understand that no child or adult should be saddled with guilt. Years after, Dolly got a call on the phone from a solicitor who asked for Mr. Savage and she replied, "He died and I don't know whether to look up to find him or down."

When Margaret misbehaved which she was always prone to do, her mother would declare that she was "just like Jim Savage!" Though she did not really know her father, she would behave like "her father" to annoy her mother.

At four years old, Moggy rode with her mother and Aunt Mamie to Dover which was in Delaware to pick up Mama who had stayed with a friend for a few days. Mother kept telling her in the back seat, "When we get there, you will be a good little girl, won't you?"

"Well, I think I will say 'shit' when we get there," not yet able to pronounce her words properly but yes, able to be mischievous. Mother begged and pleaded and yet all through dinner, Moggy looked over at her and would slip in, "I'm going to say it!"

That little mind was always churning from early on. When she was quite small, barely talking age, the preacher came to the house to baptize Margaret. When he splashed the water on her head, she declared, "You are going to make me catch my death of cold!"

Papa went to church each Sunday, a small Methodist church just five miles from the farm at Silver Beach. Dolly would go when she was home on weekends and of course,

Margaret went. One Sunday sitting by her, seven year old Margaret heard the preacher preaching on and on about divorce to which Margaret asked in her loudest voice, "Is he talking about us, Mother?" Fortunately, Dolly had her father's sense of humor and devilment so she laughed right out loud as did a few others.

Any child who attended the church every Sunday all year got a big round pin to wear in recognition. Margaret wanted one of those pins and she got one. When she found out the following year the reward was a bar to hang from the pin, her ambition waned. Her cousin Bob's did not. He had so many bars hanging from his pin, Margaret called him "General Bob."

A RURAL AREA IN THE 1940'S PROVIDED MOGGY WITH A different childhood than the suburban neighborhood we grew up in the 1960's and where she, Miss Savage, taught. We walked out of our front doors of our house-lined streets to find a dozen or more children skateboarding or riding bikes, throwing the football or organizing a game of ball. There were enough kids for a game of softball, breaking a neighbor's front window on occasion and without hysteria. Dogs ran free and chased cars which slowed down for them. Grandmas and cousins would come to visit but often lived far away. It was a nice place to grow up though there was a sameness Moggy did not experience.

A rural childhood might seem lonely but in reality, leaves room for inventiveness and adaptability with fewer people of a wider range along with wide open spaces between them. Moggy also understood hard work and focusing on what was important, essential when raising animals and working the land.

Since Margaret spent her childhood with her grandparents on their farm, she also worked on the farm. Papa sold sodas and food to the people working in the fields for the same price he had paid, including to Margaret. Working all day, she got out of hand and drank so many sodas and ate so much cheese, bologna, and moon pies, she made fifty cents but spent sixty cents. Mostly, she had blistered shoulders even with a shirt on from working in the sun all day. Each vegetable had its own particulars, so she also finished her days with some understanding of farming.

Margaret had begged to join in with what became her least favorite vegetable to work with, green beans. Picking green beans was harder for her than expected. Picking only one tall basket in a day for fifty cents was not worth it. She never wanted to see another one of those baskets again and to this day, will not pick a green bean.

Picking tomatoes was not much better. The green vines released a chemical from little hair-like glands with an objectionable sticky sugar substance which got all over her hands and arms and did not easily wash off. The trick was to break open a green tomato and run the insides over her hands and arms to relieve the itch.

As she got older, she helped Papa load the baskets of tomatoes onto the truck to take to town. She would help Papa pick these weird greenish, yellowish, pinkish tomatoes and wondered who in the world would eat them. They would wrap them in a thin tissue paper and pack them into special baskets to go to the city. Margaret was never one to eat a tomato that would ripen on its way to its destination. Most tomatoes today are most likely pumped with a gas to ripen and redden them. Growing them on the farm meant enjoying the real taste of tomatoes right off the vine.

The vine-ripened tomatoes they sold would go directly to

the canning factory. Years later when visiting a canning factory to buy a case of tomatoes, Margaret had to select a label which also dictated the price. She selected the least expensive "No Label" tomatoes knowing where they had come from, knowing they were all the same tomatoes.

Sweet potato plants grew on vines in long beds covered in a thin white material, still getting sun. Cleverly, the vines were then taken and planted using a planter pulled by two horses with a driver who sat on a seat on top of a huge barrel filled with water. Two men sat on each side on seats close to the ground with their legs straight out in front of them. Each had a one foot by two-foot tray of sweet potato vines. One would put one vine in root side down and then the other would put one in alternating until all the rows were planted. As they planted, cultivator blades would close the dirt around them and then water from the barrel would come down on the newly planted vines.

Papa would never let his granddaughter do this work though she wanted to. Later, when the vines grew and needed to be cultivated, Margaret had her job in place. The vines had to be turned towards one row so the other row could be cultivated, back and forth. This was a monotonous job done with a stick. Papa would sit on a basket at the end of the row and he had to pay Margaret five cents per row before she went on to the next row. If Papa ran out of nickels, he had to walk home to get more or Margaret would sit down and refuse to work. This was cheaper than paying Tom or Uncle Buck big money to turn vines.

Papa kept money in a huge four feet tall and three feet wide bank safe in the hall of the farmhouse. Margaret loved to twist all the dials which drove Papa nuts, of course. Anyway, she made money on the farm turning sweet potato vines.

Margaret never worked with the Irish potatoes on the farm unless Mama wanted some fresh ones for supper and sent Margaret to pull up the green plants and dig the potatoes out. She knew they gave all the tiny ones to the pigs and today going to the grocery store buying tiny potatoes, she thinks, "Make a pig of yourself."

Uncle Buck plowed up potatoes and the farm workers dug them out of the dirt, threw them in piles, and later put them in baskets. They were paid by the basket. Margaret and the farm workers' children would have potato chucking contests getting yelled at to stop. Potato chucking was fun but those potatoes meant money with none to spare.

They also grew onions that required the use of a sharp knife to cut the tops off, then piled the onions, and later placed them in sacks to be shipped. Papa was what would be called "a truck farmer" as he would take the produce by truck to Exmore and the dealers there would buy and ship it in larger trucks usually to Baltimore, Philadelphia, or New York City.

Corn grown on the farm was mostly for feeding the horses and cows. They ate not only the corn but also the fodder from the corn stalks and the dried leaves. Margaret gave them a try but not so good. The young, tender corn from the roasting ears was memorable. To this day, she cleans corn by cutting the larger end off and peeling everything easily down, including the silks. This works better than starting at the narrower end peeling back to the stalk end. Just a little nugget of wisdom from a farmer's granddaughter.

An interesting, less common root vegetable, fennel, grew wild on the farm. Margaret's job was to cut it to ship to the city where it was appreciated most with eel. Yes, eel. Who would want to eat eel, she asked herself? Once as an adult visiting Mexico City, Margaret ordered a soup with what looked like small noodles that turned out to be baby eel. Refusing to eat this soup meant being hungry that evening, no doubt. Eel soup did not go very well with Brandy Alexanders anyhow.

Though Margaret grew up on the Eastern Shore of Virginia on a farm far away from the need or desire for travel, as an adult, she did travel. Years after her introduction to eel with fennel from the farm, she traveled to Amsterdam and witnessed fishermen taking eel off their boats for local restaurants. And there they were again, on menus.

Margaret loved picking strawberries best. She could crawl down the strawberry patch on her knees and pick one hundred quarts of strawberries in a morning which she did every year on picking days. Payment was by tickets with "J.R. Kilmon" on each one turned in for money at the end of the morning. On occasion, Margaret would sneak off the school bus in the mornings at other strawberry fields because she could make ten dollars a morning by picking strawberries which was better than going to school. She would then read until the school bus came back in the afternoon. No one told on her, including the school bus driver.

Strawberries remain a favorite for daiquiris, cold soups, strawberry pies, and of course, eating on cereal, but they are often not raised locally like they used to be which is sad. The local strawberries in season today are a whole five dollars per quart.

Back then, a crate of fresh, local strawberries held twenty-four quarts. The crates were driven to a shed known as the strawberry block where buyers sat and bid for these freshly picked berries, the prettier ones bringing more money. Moggy always helped Papa place the prettiest berries on top. This very good idea may have sparked a very bad idea.

There was a line of about forty fig trees separating their

property from the Marron's property. Each fall season, they picked sweet, tender and ripe figs and shipped them to the city. Figs are a pain to pick as the milk from the stems begins to make the thumb and nail hurt. Margaret Anne had a great idea since there were onions growing next to the line of fig trees. She first filled each of her quarts with two or three onions and topped them off with figs which made a crate in no time. Instead of this crate going to the city, a lady from town bought it to make preserves. Papa proudly told her he had a really pretty crate picked by his little granddaughter. The woman paid and left... and returned in two hours. She did not come back for more figs. Papa's cry was for Mama to do something! Margaret Anne needed to stick with strawberry picking.

She never saved any of the "J.R. Kilmon" strawberry picking tickets from her childhood but managed later in life to find some at a flea market from another farmer, "Cecil Johnson." Margaret gave a couple of them to dear friends, Caro and Butch Doughty, who live in Louisiana and have a museum of items from the Eastern Shore including one of Mama's old irons. Special doesn't describe it.

As if the farm work didn't keep everybody busy enough, they also maintained a garden of watermelons, cantaloupe, butterbeans, radishes, beets and more which, guessing correctly, Margaret sold at the beach. She continued to be clever about income opportunities on the farm. By age eight, each morning all summer, she loaded her wagon with fresh picked vegetables and trolleyed them down to the rented beach cottages. The concept of "vacation" escaped this eight AM merchant. She was on a mission to sell her goods going down the row of waterfront cottages knocking on doors, followed by the two rows of cottages back behind, swinging around again for another knock at the doors until all the produce sold.

Cousin Bob had moved nearby late one summer in time to help by pulling the wagon. Thrifty Margaret would offer Bob his choice of dime or nickel in payment and not having the concept of "conservation of matter," Bob would pick the nickel leaving Margaret with not only a little extra money but also a clear conscience not having cheated him.

In the 1930's and 40's, farmers helped each other out and shared equipment. One time, Papa was visiting with the neighbors and Mama and Margaret were home and this truck came by buying scrap metal for the war effort. Margaret saw another opportunity to make money and to help with the war effort. At age nine or ten, she did not recognize farming equipment from scrap metal and loaded them up with a lot of Papa's good farming equipment. Papa was much too into running his mouth rather than working, according to Mama, and Margaret was into money-making opportunities, a bad combination in this case. As much as Papa liked to talk, Margaret liked to make money, and to spend, not save, the money she made.

Farming was hard in ways and not all it was cracked up to be. Some farmers rented land from each other creating a few miles distance between crops which was always a challenge. Some years were bad with too much rain and crops got washed out, some too little rain, and sometimes there would be plain crop failure. With no money coming in and no back up, those working on the farm still had to be paid. This created worry, but they managed.

With all the responsibilities at home on the farm, Mama and Papa did not take vacations. Ocean City, Maryland was less than one and a half hours north and each year, once or twice, they would drive up for the day to meet Papa's family for a huge picnic. Margaret would get to go to Marty's Playland. There was a slot to put money in and a movie star's photo came out. Margaret hated to get Clark Gable's due to his icky mustache, or Mickey Rooney just because she didn't care for him. Marty's Playland is still open in Ocean City and Margaret still goes there.

Margaret remembers well when a big change came in the way of a letter from the government dictating that Papa had to plant soybeans. He cried. He really did cry because he wanted to grow what he wanted to grow. They were his fields he had always had control over. Papa gave up farming rather than go along with the dictates of the government and began renting his land to farmers who went along with the dictates. Papa had worked hard and loved farming.

Papa also harvested oysters in the colder months. It was a well-known fact not to eat oysters in the summertime but only when months had an "R" in them, September through April. The oysters grow fatter and healthier during the cooler months and perhaps there is less bacteria in the water.

Papa had oyster grounds in the creek to one side of their farm. Oyster grounding is best in protected, shallow, salty-to-brackish waters where oysters remain close to the bottom. Papa "planted" oysters and "harvested" them with oyster tongs like eight-foot tall scissors. After tonging, he used a culling hammer to separate the good oysters from the smaller ones not yet ready and planted those back in the oyster grounds.

Oysters were always in great demand bringing in both income and opportunities to socialize. Papa was always having oyster roasts for people. The oysters would roast on a large piece of chicken wire over a giant fire Papa built. Nothing else was served but butter, hot sauces and vinegar, pepper and crackers, and sometimes bourbon, all to everyone's delight and satisfaction.

When Mama wanted to cook some for the family, she sent Margaret with a set of tongs out on the boat at the oyster grounds. Margaret's cat, Midnight, made for good company following her down with eating oysters in his mind. Margaret would break open a few oysters for Midnight. When Papa passed away, several people came to bid on his oyster grounds. It was a no-no to ever trespass on anyone else's grounds.

Papa also had a fishing pound with a long line of tall poles extending out into the bay to the seven-or-eight-foot watermark. Nets were stretched along this line of poles and at the end was a huge circle of poles with nets. Fish would swim along the line of nets and then enter the giant circle.

Papa went to the pound each morning during the winter to pull fish in to sell. Margaret was never allowed to go to the fish pound for fear she would fall over pulling the nets. Papa might have fallen over pulling the nets, as well, and he might not have been able to swim either. He wore big heavy boots down to the fishing pound. Tangier Island sits in the Chesapeake Bay north of Silver Beach and men from Tangier came in the winter, lived on their boats, and found work with Papa.

Papa would not mess with crabs. Instead, the family ate lots of fish, certainly lots of vegetables, and the chickens they raised which also meant plenty of eggs. Margaret did not know about beef or steak in the 1940's, not until going to college.

3

CATCH A MISCHIEVOUS MOMENT

School began with first grade in this country back in the 1940's, not just on the Eastern Shore. Kindergarten was not yet in place though napping at school like a kindergartener was. Margaret was not used to taking naps as she had not been conditioned to. Mama always told Margaret she did not have to take naps if she didn't want to so she did not. In the middle of the day after lunch in first grade, the teacher insisted that she lie down like all the other students on this ratty old rug rolled out each day. No nap time for Margaret meant no nap time for anyone around her. She was always rolling around, poking and kicking others to wake them up. This may have been the first of a long history of established school routines Margaret threw overboard, and so young. It was in her nature and she sure had fun with it from the very beginning.

There were a string of times Margaret took off when preparing to start school which proved to be early warning signs. Dolly and Ronnie's mother, Madge, took their children together for their first school physicals. Ronnie went first because he was the meanest and supposedly the bravest but when they finished his vaccinations, he ran out yelling for Moggy to get out of there, they were going to kill her! Their mothers had to chase after the two down the street. Moggy did get her vaccinations and did enter school at age six.

Dolly decided Margaret also should have "a permanent" because her hair was fairly straight. Since Dolly was working, she asked her good friend to take Margaret to the local beauty parlor. At that time in history, to get "a perm," they used something likened to a beehive with wires hanging down. Margaret looked at that thing and thought she might be subject to a brain wave test so she took off down the street and Mary had to chase her down. Mary took Margaret with still-straight hair back to Dolly expressing that Margaret was one bad child who could also run really fast.

Dolly also took Margaret for a dental checkup. The local dentist was a tiny little man who had machinery that looked like it came from the Middle Ages. He got Margaret into the chair, proceeded to determine that she had a cavity, and proceeded with the grinder tool. Margaret was not happy, of course, and then the dentist escalated the situation by calling her "Lizzie." Lizzie was a relative not highly regarded due to her mean streak. It was at that moment Margaret bit the dentist and ran out to the waiting room. Her mother was trying to understand what was wrong when Margaret said, "He called me 'Wizzie!'"

Apparently, that was all Dolly needed to know. The dentist appeared and announced in the waiting room what a bad child she was. Margaret, in truth, enjoyed her notoriety. This same misbehavior, or perhaps mischievousness, carried over into school and it all played into not liking school.

Having to walk a mile to meet the bus and then ride

twelve miles on the bus to get to school didn't help. Mama had taught Margaret to read so there was no place in her life for "Mother and Father," "Dick and Jane," and "Puff and Spot" in the first grade primers. She quickly figured out that was a bunch of hooey. "Mother and Father" in those little books never argued, and "Dick and Jane" were such absolutely good children. They bored her more every day so what did Margaret do?

In the school rhythm band, the noisiest instrument, the cymbals would have been Margaret's preference, but the least noisy triangles were assigned to this mischievous young lady. Margaret found her way around that. Though she was not allowed to play with the building blocks, she knew exactly the main blocks to knock down the fort as fellow students were crawling through the tunnels they had built.

Her cousin, Nancy, with the same devilish blood, was in her class and they together created some action getting themselves into some trouble. Once, Nancy brought her brother's boxing gloves to school and Nancy knocked Margaret out as Margaret was putting her glove on. Nancy was quick to hide her glove and Margaret was the one who got into trouble.

Was Margaret bad? Was she seeking attention? Or was she yearning for a more creative teacher? When she taught, she aimed to be that more creative teacher. Looking back, she hopes she was. And yes, I can say, she was. Not easily sitting quietly in class as a student herself, she was comfortable with her own students moving about.

I recall she spent no time in her chair at her desk and little time standing in front of our class. Miss Savage would sit atop the radiator ledge along the windows or anywhere else she wanted to sit to interact with the class. And she chewed gum and did not hide it either. We never even thought about chewing gum and we did behave for Miss Savage. She was never uptight so we were not which set the tone for a creative classroom. We grew up in a tumultuous decade that ended on an upswing, the summer before our sixth grade year in Miss Savage's class, Apollo 11 landed on the moon, July 20, 1969.

During Margaret's first year of school, Pearl Harbor in Hawaii was attacked, December 7, 1941. On that very day, Margaret had gone with her grandparents to visit dear friends in Laurel, Delaware. They had a huge house and a huge radio that actually worked. As they were listening to the radio, the announcement come on that the Japanese had bombed Pearl Harbor, clearly terrible. In her mind, not knowing where Pearl Harbor was and not wanting to remain there with those oh-so-proper people, Margaret grew concerned. Was Pearl Harbor on their way home? They did safely return home from Laurel to Silver Beach in the expected three and a half hours, a drive that would today be a mere one and a half hours.

Second grade was as unremarkable as first grade for Margaret. Being able to read along with a sure lack of enthusiasm for school lead to increasingly more successful attempts at staying home. Third grade was different. Billy was Margaret's best friend in class that year and they were the only two children who brought lunch from home. Mrs. Henry was their teacher. She and her husband owned the local five and dime store. What more could a person want if they owned the five and dime? Mrs. Henry had everything, even a sandwich toaster she brought to school to toast Billy's and Margaret's sandwiches. It was like being at the drug store minus the Coca-Colas.

Nancy got to be a patrol that year wearing that shiny patrol badge. Did Margaret get to be a patrol that year? No, she did not. Why would anyone obey her? She did get to wear that badge, however, by promising Nancy a candy bar in exchange for wearing that badge. This might have been third grade, but Margaret knew her economics. She buried the badge and told Nancy to bring her two candy bars to get the badge back.

Third grade meant plowing through a grammar workbook which meant, of course, Margaret hid hers in the back of the file cabinet until she heard rumor that somebody was going to fail if that grammar book was not completed. So that some-body dug the grammar book out and completed it in three days. Mrs. Henry was a kind and patient teacher, never raising her voice, a good lesson for Margaret when she became a teacher. Owning the five and dime may have seemed like enough but being loved by her students meant so much more, all good memories from third grade with Mrs. Henry.

FOURTH GRADE MEANT HAVING TO MEMORIZE THE STATES AND their capitals, a cluttering of the mind Margaret refused. These were early warning signs that Margaret believed in being true to oneself. Nancy stood up and said all of hers perfectly and then Margaret stood up and stared at the ceiling telling the teacher since Nancy had been looking up at the ceiling, the states and capitals must have been written up there for them to read out loud. That did it, but the students who were brave enough laughed. It was worth it. Margaret loved getting a laugh.

The only art project in all of fourth grade was to make a brown and white plaster of paris collie dog head using a mold. Students had to bring in five cents to make one and Margaret got her money in, always eager to make these sorts of gifts for Mama. While this was an escape from otherwise uninteresting schoolwork, Margaret threw the brown and white idea overboard and painted hers green and blue and yellow. Maybe there had not been enough brown paint left but maybe there had been.

Mama faithfully put the colorful collie heads Margaret made on display but without felt on the bottom, the furniture over the years was covered in white scratch marks. Making plaster of paris collie heads was a success while memorizing states and capitals was not. Margaret refused to memorize anything of no consequence and that was that. There is a good chance the only thing she learned that year was that making anything from a mold was not really art.

That same year, Margaret often stayed after school for punishment and when she had the money, she would pay to make more plaster of paris collie dog heads. Because the Eastern Shore was safe and people were kind, Margaret could hitchhike home. There were no "late buses." She rode the twelve miles on hay wagons, trucks, tractors, and in occasional cars.

Margaret was surrounded by wonderful people to learn from along with Mama and Papa. School for her remained dull in comparison and didn't have the potential to get any better. There was one thing about school that she loved most and that was reading. Margaret read everything she could get her hands on.

The one other thing she loved in school was construction paper. She would move mountains at Halloween time to get another piece of orange construction paper to make Mama another pumpkin. Christmastime was all about the green and red construction paper chains. Those were the things that were fun, along with entertaining everyone with stories and antics.

Between fourth and fifth grade, Dolly remarried and

moved to Norfolk in an area of Virginia known as Hampton Roads. After divorcing Jim Savage, she and a boyfriend from growing up rekindled their relationship. He was a wealthy man owning part of a large brewery, a trucking line, and if that wasn't enough, a hotel. Though a mere seventy miles from their hometown of Exmore on the Eastern Shore, a long ferry ride was necessary to reach Norfolk.

The Chesapeake Bay Bridge Tunnel was not yet in place. Completed in 1964, its construction took over three years. The seventeen and a half mile long alternating tunnels and causeways finally connected the southern tip of the Eastern Shore to Hampton Roads but not until Margaret had moved away.

Margaret's fifth grade teacher, Mrs. Nottingham, was her favorite teacher and she was beautiful. Dolly and Mrs. Nottingham were best of friends. When Dolly came to visit from Norfolk, all the children thought she was a movie star. Dolly was very pretty, always driving a fancy car and wearing a beautiful fur coat.

Margaret would on occasion visit her mother in Norfolk and once she ran away, took the ferry back to the Eastern Shore, and hitchhiked back to Mama and Papa. She learned something from that marriage. Money is not important and without love, money is no substitute. Dolly seemed to have everything but happiness.

Her stepfather was too about himself and Margaret knew by a feeling that Mama and Papa didn't like him either. In fact, she felt certain her mother didn't care for him. He was not a kind man. Her stepfather would rather give Margaret money to take a friend to the movies or the soda fountain to get her out of the house and away from Dolly. Anything but being around him was fine with her. Once on a trip to Niagara

Falls and Quebec City, he would not allow Dolly and Margaret to stand beside each other to take a photograph.

A favorite time in Norfolk was going to see The Freedom Train, a seven-car train which traveled across the country in the late 1940's dedicated to sharing some of America's most valued historical documents and the history of American democracy. Dolly and her husband took Margaret to see the train but the line was horrendous. Margaret could have waited but because her stepfather could not, he attempted to bribe an officer to cut in line and almost got put in jail. The thought of him being in jail was better than seeing those documents on The Freedom Train.

The marriage lasted four years and then Dolly came home to the Eastern Shore later dating a nice man with the last name of Savage, no relation. Margaret respected this Mr. Savage more than her own father and certainly more than her stepfather. This Mr. Savage's wife had passed away and Margaret became good friends with his children. Though her mother did seem to love him, they never married, simply enjoying each other's company and being best of friends.

WHEN VISITING MARGARET'S CLASS, DOLLY SEEMED TO GIVE more attention to the teacher or to the other kids in the class. And she gave more attention to her own friends. Being "just like" her father, she understood, might not be a good thing. It was more about seeking attention by misbehaving which carried over in many ways. On Sundays, Dolly and her friends would sit together on their towels at the beach. Margaret would yell, "Watch me! Watch how long I can stay under!"

Dolly would be watching and Margaret would go under

the water and stay and stay until her lungs felt like they were
exploding and she couldn't stand it any longer. When she
would pop up, no one was watching. She did this again and
again and always, the same thing would happen. Was Dolly
not worried about Margaret's swimming abilities? Or, if she
didn't watch, maybe the stunt wasn't there in front of her? All
her daughter was seeking was attention. Had Mama been
there, she would have watched.

Years later when she taught, Miss Savage gave each
student her attention so they would not misbehave or show
off to get attention. It actually worked because all anyone
wants is a bit of notice for something neat, exciting, or important to them. Miss Savage knew making a big thing, or at
least something, was more important than no-thing at all. She
had few, maybe no discipline problems because that old
attention thing was important in her class. Perhaps, too, there
were no discipline problems because she had *been there and
done that* and knew how to head those problems off at the
pass.

Sixth grade for Margaret was a slump year. The sixth
grade teacher had this ugly ceramic swan up high on a tall
bookshelf and Margaret broke it playing indoor ball. Was it
an accident? Was she supposed to be playing ball? It's a toss-
up. Shooting fellow sixth graders with water by leaning way
over past her desk to put her finger on the water spigot was
definitely no accident.

There were incidents at school around sixth grade
Margaret would never forget. Aunt Mamie had stayed in
Newport News, Virginia and married after business school.
She and her husband, Uncle Buck White, moved home to
help Papa farm after Ducca passed away. They built a home
on the farm property which was when their son, Cousin Bob,

became Margaret's best companion. Caesar's triumvirate, his board of rulers, would not have been a match for the two of them. They loved each other like brother and sister and no one could pick on Bob with Margaret there. Once, Bob got on the front seat of the school bus, just six years old at the time, and a lady asked who he thought he was taking her daughter's seat.

Bob stood up and said, "I think I am a boy!"

Margaret stood up and cheered and said, "He is and he will sit there!" And he did! All adventures back then included Bob. They love each other to this day and speak often though he lives in California.

Other memories from sixth grade not easily erased involved Eddie, a classmate who still lives at Silver Beach. He and Margaret were playing a game with a pencil, one of those yellow number 2 wooden pencils with the sharp lead point. Spreading her fingers out, hand flat on the desk, Eddie had to rapidly bang the pencil tip down between each of her fingers without missing. Missing would mean the lead tip of the pencil would impale Margaret's finger and that's exactly what it did. All these years later, Margaret finally had that piece of lead removed. The memories with Eddie remain.

One day, Eddie came in quite late after recess. The teacher was mad and asked him why and he said, "I was looking for my nickel."

She asked, "Why couldn't you find it?"

He retorted, "Because it was lost!"

Would Margaret's burst of laughter at this surprise anyone? She was kept inside for recess the following day along with Eddie. Not only was she kept inside but her report card grades on the conduct side were usually U's. She told Mama "U" stood for "Unusual" and not "Unsatisfactory."

Mama told her it wasn't important and that is what Margaret lived by. Perfect grades and perfect conduct were never her thing as life held too much else important like reading and music and animals, having a good time in one's own skin, and loving life.

Mrs. Nottingham was her teacher again in seventh grade, guaranteeing another good year. Always kind and forgiving, Mrs. Nottingham greatly influenced how Margaret herself taught. A little laughter and kindness can make a big difference in the mind of a child.

Having attended many of Mrs. Nottingham's birthday parties, Margaret always told her how she had impacted Margaret's life. Margaret had a chance to thank her for being so kind to her and to Charles, two children in the class without fathers. A tear ran down her cheek, tears ran down both of Margaret's cheeks, wetter than wet. She developed a treasured friendship over the years with Virginia Nottingham and recently stood by her bedside after she suffered a stroke. Gigi was one hundred years old.

WALKING HOME FROM THE SCHOOL BUS IN EARLY JUNE AFTER Sanie and Nick's concession stand opened, Margaret would go the extra distance to stop and get a candy bar. Once, she walked a mile further almost home when she discovered that Nick had given her five cents too much change so she turned around and walked back to the beach to return the nickel. Nick was so pleased with Margaret, he bragged about her. From very young, her grandparents had instilled honesty in her and she knew the value of a nickel.

Later when she taught, she wanted to instill in her students the same honesty. Whenever they found a nickel, dime, or quarter on the playground, she would have them put it in a piece of paper adding their name and the date and take it to the school office. After two weeks, if not claimed, the money was theirs to keep. In all thirty-three years of teaching, to her knowledge, never was anything ever stolen from her class.

Yes, one time a foreign dollar bill was passed around the class and was taken. Miss Savage appealed to all of the students to please return it but no one did. There was a solution. Everyone, including the teacher, put their heads down and closed their eyes and whoever had the dollar was to fold it in a wad and throw it as far as possible. With all heads down and eyes closed, Pop! It appeared. Miss Savage was the most happy of all, and someone remained innocent.

Another time, a guest speaker who with her mother had escaped Russia with only their lives and a few valuables sewn into their coat lining shared a Faberge ring with the class. She insisted on passing the jewel around so thirty-four children could get a close look. Miss Savage's heart was in her throat but the ring made it around the whole class and back. What a wonderful chance to hold a beautiful Faberge treasure. Margaret kept her own treasures over the years including to this very day, some of the musical instruments she acquired as a child.

Papa's Boston Pops listening routine on Sunday afternoon radio perhaps began Margaret's love of music. And Mama would sing to her, often religious songs, while in the back porch swing and quite often during a thunderstorm. *"Beautiful, beautiful brown eyes"* was perhaps in memory of Mr. Fletcher, her first husband who had died. Mama would sing about the white cliffs of Dover which was confusing to this little person because they had visited Dover, Delaware and there were no white cliffs there. Still playing Mama's songs on her guitar today, Margaret loves them all, even the song about Dover which is in England.

Dolly played the piano like Mama did and was also quite good. She played and sang ragtime of sorts and had quite a repertoire of songs with the ukulele. Some were naughty but as most children, Margaret knew best ones like *Camptown Races* which was cleaner... "*Bet my money on a bob tailed nag, who's gonna bet on the bay ...*"

Even her father helped create a music memory early in her life. Her parents took her to Chincoteague, an island of few people in the Atlantic Ocean just off the coast of the Eastern Shore. The island is known for wild ponies and a children's book called *Misty of Chincoteague* written in 1947. For Margaret, Chincoteague was known for wild Savages of the father and uncle type. While there, she went out to play with some of those wild Savage offspring who introduced her to their wilderness by tying her to a tree.

Left there crying until her mother found her, she cried all the way home and remembers the only song her father ever sang to her, "*Amapola... my pretty little poppy... yo te quiero amada nina mia...*" Had she known as a small child the translation, "I love you, my dear child," this song sung by her father would have been more dear. On her guitar, she plays this song even today but chooses not to think of being tied to a tree, nor does she sing.

Once as a child walking across a ball field, a hard ball bounced once and caught Margaret in the throat. She could not talk at all for a whole month giving Mama and Papa a break. Fortunately, her voice recovered but her ability to sing did not.

Margaret's musical instrument of choice beginning in upper elementary years was the accordion so her mother and grandparents pitched in and got her one. She not only taught herself to play but became good enough to play at Sunday evening church concerts along The Shore. Dolly loved taking her and showing her off. Just before college, she dropped playing her accordion, but not before playing on the local radio, *Tales from the Vienna Woods* by Johann Strauss II.

The Lawrence Welk Show aired on television from 1955 to 1971. Myron Florin performed with his accordion on the show and Margaret was no Myron Florin though she was also known, at least around her hometown, to be a quite good accordion player. She has kept her accordion and still enjoys classical music to this day.

ONCE MARGARET REACHED HIGH SCHOOL AGE, DOLLY WENT to work for Benjamin's, another family-owned and much larger store. Margaret got the job of gift-wrapping at Christmastime and bookkeeping tasks which she enjoyed. Dolly later went to work for an oil company doing bookkeeping and even taxes for several business in town.

Feeling she did not fit in, Dolly had left high school and gone with her sister, Mamie, to business college in Newport News near Norfolk. She loved it and built on her knowledge all her life. Dolly taught her daughter a strong work ethic and independence, and even taught her to do her own taxes which she does herself to this very day. Dolly was smart and clever and loved by everyone. She taught Margaret to make work fun which influenced how Margaret approached teaching. And like Papa, her mother taught her to enjoy playing jokes on people, all in fun.

Even in high school, Margaret managed to "win" in discipline rounds. She had study hall in the library with her old friend, Ronnie, and a girl a year below them. The librarian who was not married flirted unmercifully with a supervisor who would come by. Knowing that supervisor was married, Margaret, even at that age, did not approve of such behavior. While the librarian was out in the hallway flirting with the supervisor, she got her two friends to help her turn as many books on the shelf as possible upside down. They managed to flip five hundred books and naturally, Margaret got caught as the instigator.

Her punishment was to spend her lunch hour in the principal's office for one solid week which was no punishment at all. Intended to embarrass her and make her repentant, instead she took the opportunity to wave at everyone and put on a little one-hour show at the office plate glass window. Margaret did fill her schedule with everything she could. She preferred literature and music, threw in typing and home economics, and took all the college prep classes she needed to include the sciences.

Margaret was the only girl in physics class and burned up every motor she could. When Dolly started getting billed, that experimentation stopped though the antics clearly did not. In biology class, the walls were lined with shelves containing a huge collection of ugly specimen containers. Quite often, Margaret would take the specimens off the shelves and place them on desks before classmates arrived. When they arrived, they would make squeamish shrieks at the ugly specimens.

She kept getting caught doing this and the punishment was to write these long words five hundred times, or maybe even a thousand. Dolly entered the punishment phase again but this time, she taught her daughter to tape five or six pencils together to write the words much faster. The teacher never catching on to this neat game was a disappointment and Margaret never stopped placing specimens on desks until the last day of class.

Margaret carried the biology pranks over into the required biology class she took in college. She and her not-so-humored lab partner had their own little frog to dissect and Margaret needed more action. Margaret's students over the years would certainly remember her unabashed love of chewing gum. Back in college during the frog dissection in biology class, the Dentyne gum came in handy. She bundled up a bit of the wad into a lovely little shape and inserted it into the frog.

She called the professor over to relate how she could not find that lovely pink organ in the diagram they were given. He was perplexed and called over his assistant for consultation. They poked and prodded a bit, never figured this out, and thankfully went no farther. Margaret's sense of fun never ended as she imagined the Science Digest article, "Frog Swallows Tiny Piece of Dentyne Gum."

Going to parties and cheerleading made Margaret a very normal high school girl. Softball was her sport of choice from grade school through high school and this young girl was good at it. She could catch a ball like she could catch a mischievous moment. Her throwing arm did not serve her as well and headed more quickly in later life towards arthritis.

Margaret was never crazy about sports which in later life manifested itself in one of her greatest fears, watching a baseball game heading beyond nine innings. Not much into spectator sports, particularly on the television, she would keep up with the Baltimore Ravens only to keep up with social conversation. Why? The Raven's mascot is "neat."

Margaret avoided struggling through foreign language classes by getting them waved at the risk of finding them necessary for college entry. They were not, but algebra was. Memorizing formulas did not suit her so exam time, she knew, meant failing. Starting in on all that memorization bogged her down until a miracle happened. The preacher's son who was older and good at algebra sat near her and he held his paper up as he was taking his exam such that Margaret could see every little thing. She had never, ever cheated on anything or copied anything but since this was the preacher's son, she felt that "God has sent me a sign" so she put it all down on her own paper and "successfully" completed algebra class.

Once, she handed in ten pages of science notes for a history project and got an "A" on it. Later as a teacher, Margaret would put a personal note in her lesson plans turned in to the principal to see if the principal really did review the lesson plans. She always read her own students' work and would answer a note put in to her from a student. Margaret knew enough from her own behavior growing up how to keep up and keep ahead for the benefit of her students.

High school was also about paying other students to make her blouse or apron or whatever in home economics class. Neither she nor her mother could sew though even ten years before her mother passed away, they bought a sewing machine which didn't work. Dolly took a hammer to it which knocked the bobbin winder off.

That should have ended sewing but as an adult, Margaret connected with her father and they decided to attempt sewing. He tried to mend a hole in the seat of Margaret's expensive pair of madras plaid slacks. The mend went up the whole leg causing Margaret to walk like a Charlie Chaplin slap stick comedy act. Then her father washed those beautiful slacks that shrunk to the size to fit a Barbie doll. Sewing should never have been a part of any of their lives as Margaret learned back in high school.

Margaret's own unique brand of folly, as anyone could tell, continuously wove its way throughout school and beyond. In defense of her judgement on appropriate school behavior, she did defend one high school teacher her fellow students did not like. When they were hard on the teacher, Margaret was even nicer to her jumping right in to defend her. Kindness always did and always would redeem Margaret Savage.

SPORTS-AVOIDANCE KICKED IN MOST AFTER HIGH SCHOOL. Being required to take physical education classes in college, Margaret learned more about how to avoid them. Archery was out of the question because anyone overseeing the selection of physical education classes knew not to put bows and arrows in her hands. Bows and arrows can hurt people.

She managed her way into fencing class and pinned the teacher against the wall a few times, unleashing any general or vague personal feelings of anger. She was no "Captain from Castile." A 1947 feature film, *Captain from Castile* was about an escape from the Spanish Inquisition into the expedition to conquer Mexico, which clearly involved excellent sword skills. Fencing went out in Margaret's life with the likes of old movies going out. Who has ever heard of *Captain from Castile*? Margaret must have a very good memory.

She remembers well finding herself in the National Folk Dance in the senior dance class as a freshman in college. She does not remember how she managed to survive in that class, feeling like a pet monkey that could never learn the steps. Refusing to buy special shoes for the class, she instead painted her saddle oxfords white. Noticing the red soles of those painted-white shoes, her teacher grabbed her by the ear and took her to the front of the class for a "don't be like this person" lesson.

Why would any teacher berate such cleverness? Once a

teacher, she would never, but rather found humor in the moment and appreciation for her own students' ingenuity. Margaret was the student who felt fortunate to earn a D in a class, as opposed to failing. Grades remained unimportant to her. Making the best of any situation was important to her. "Unlimited cuts from class" was her go-ahead incentive to ever seek A's. Incentives, incentives!

After the first five or six lessons, she discovered how to play the nine-hole golf course nine times in one day in order to pass golf class. Aha! Incentive! Margaret arrived at the golf course at seven AM one morning with about thirty-six golf balls and hit all of them to the first hole, losing a very few before going on to the second hole. By dark, she returned to her dorm having completed the golf class passing with a B or C which was good enough. Badminton, next, became a balcony sport. With a balcony nearby, Margaret deliberately hit the birdie onto the balcony to get a break from playing badminton.

Participating in sports barely followed her throughout her life. Stationary bike riding, not going anywhere past her cell phone or wrist watch, suits her to this day along with walking, particularly along the beach. And today, please no games of Bridge, and sometimes Uno or Phase Ten though unfortunately, boredom does lead to cheating and a good laugh about it.

The only sport Margaret never sought a break from was water skiing. Owning her own speedboat and easily finding a driver, with no grades to make and no external incentives, she enjoyed miles and miles of water skiing. Ronnie Nelson, her dearest friend for so many years who even once crawled under the cottage to get Margaret's cat, went on many adventures with her and her cousin, Bob, who also did repair jobs on her boat. Her best friend and suitemate all four years of college, "Nitti," joined them once she came along.

Once, Ronnie and Bob, Margaret and Nitti took the ferry to go dancing in Norfolk. They put hats out, Ronnie on bongo drums, Bob playing the guitar, Margaret and Nitti attempting to sing. They did well enough to pay for a night in a motel except Ronnie told the people he was Ron Nelson. He really was Ron Nelson but not the popular singer of Ozzie and Harriet fame. They didn't buy it yet on went the antics.

Ronnie, Bob, and Margaret would hitchhike to Exmore ten miles away and to get home, would buy a watermelon and stand along the road and see who would sympathize and give them and their heavy load a ride back to Silver Beach. Visiting Ocean City, Maryland, they could not follow the rules at Frontier Land, instead taking cap pistols and robbing the robbers. Any game got twisted around like that. This beach crew was bred for fun.

Some of the beach made its way to Fairfax once Margaret was teaching. The three picked up driftwood from their Eastern Shore beach and sold it to the Layton Hall Elementary community and did well. Some of the proceeds would have been spent down in Georgetown had not Ronnie and Bob been kicked out of the clubs for deciding to sing falsetto. Moggy's childhood would not have been complete without the dearest of relatives and friends through those years as the adventures went on.

Among many reasons to attend college, what Dolly said one day created one of them. Margaret was in tenth grade and went with Dolly to Exmore. One local store they called "the ten cent store." The clerk there looked to be about ninety years old, all bent over trying to sell ten cent items.

"Now Margaret Anne, when you graduate from high school, I will buy you a convertible and you can ride around in it and be very happy with it for a couple of years while you work in this store and be just like this lady or, you can go away to college and not have a convertible until you buy it yourself when you have a decent job. Remember, if you stay here, you will look like that lady one day working here at "the ten cent store" for the rest of your life." That very day, this sixteen year old chose college and one day would buy herself a convertible.

Talking with people later in life who took high school field trips from Tennessee all the way to Washington, D.C., or even to far away New York City, reminded her that their high school memories were of trips to Jamestown or Yorktown, Virginia just north of Norfolk. Her field trip memories were more of the two boys in her class creating a muddy mess fighting in a trench by the bus before returning home not too far down the road.

Margaret remains in contact with some classmates, the memory-making ones like Eddie and Tommy and Kirby from the elementary school days but never did go back for high school reunions once off to college. Why would anyone want to bring back high school? The thought of taking algebra again would be Margaret's great torment though she sure would have enjoyed burning up motors again in physics class. The high school is not there anymore anyhow.

MARGARET ATTENDED THE COLLEGE OF MARY WASHINGTON which was founded in 1908 and named after Mary Ball Washington, our first president, George Washington's mother who was a resident of the town. Fredericksburg, Virginia is an hour south of Fairfax County where George Washington's home, Mount Vernon, is located. After graduating in 1957,

Margaret spent her teaching career in an enclave of Fairfax County now called the City of Fairfax.

Her college became associated with the University of Virginia in 1944 as its women's division and became its own separate institution in 1972 when the University of Virginia became coeducational. Margaret later attended the University of Virginia and received a Master's in Audio-Visual. Hopefully, it increased her teaching salary.

Papa had died of a heart attack in 1949 while Margaret was in high school and Mama died of complications from a stroke in 1953, the summer before Margaret left home for college. During the summers of those college years,1953, 1954, and 1955, Margaret was a camp counselor in the Poconos in Pennsylvania. Any thoughts of outgrowing her fun-loving and practical joking ways learned early on from Papa are abated with camp counselor stories.

In those times, children had to "clean their plates" but no one had to ever tell Margaret to eat everything on her plate because she never put anything on her plate she did not plan to eat, not to be wasteful. Growing up during World War II was always a reminder there are hungry people in the world. One summer at camp, she was assigned a dozen seven, eight, and nine year olds and one was a tiny and thin little dear seven year old soul named Tessie.

The rule in the dining hall was to eat everything served on the plate and even Margaret, not happy with everything on her plate, ate everything to be a good example. The day came when cooked spinach showed up on everyone's plate. Margaret struggled to eat the spinach and watched everyone else bravely struggle to eat the spinach with the exception of Tessie. Tessie apparently "ate" all of her spinach until the head of the cafeteria noticed the pile of spinach on the floor.

Not being happy with her, they were going to give little

Tessie the treatment. Just as they asked, "Who did this?" Margaret called out, "I did it!"

She saw the look in Tessie's eyes that told her everything. No words were ever exchanged about the spinach but every time it was served from then on, Margaret would sneak the spinach off of Tessie's plate and eat it for her. This was a bonding sort of thing. The higher ups were not exactly pleased with Margaret's example setting so she was never sure why they hired her for three consecutive summers. She must have piqued their interest.

There were water pipes running all over the campground a half a foot above the ground, perhaps making repairing leaks easier. Running around at night, however, was more difficult as there was more tripping than running. Sure enough on her day off, Margaret bought fluorescent paint, waited until the dark of night, and with the help of friends, painted those above ground pipes. After the sun shone on them the next day, the pipes shined at night like heavenly stars. The higher ups wanted to know, "Who did it?" Margaret was never shy about saying, "I did it!" There was a string of three summers of "I did its."

The last summer, the most successful "I did it" took place in the form of "We did it!" A terribly bad hurricane caused the river to rise, the bridge to wash out, and parts of houses to have floated away. The camp community was in threat of drowning should the dam break. Margaret and company had to remain calm and assure that the children did not know of the danger. When the event was over and the children were united with their parents and all was calm, there were accolades because, "We did it!"

Margaret was unable to be a camp counselor again in 1956 because she came home conveniently "forgetting" her trunk and all her clothes so her mother sent her back to Mary

Washington to attend summer school. Margaret was always good at following the fun and that summer back at school was just that.

While in college, Margaret would go to the local Catholic church so when she went home for the holiday, she decided to tell her mother she was planning to convert. There were six or eight people sitting around the dinner table when she announced, "I am going to convert to Catholicism."

There was quiet everywhere when Dolly said, "Moggy, don't you think you'd better become a better Methodist before you start branching out?" That ended that. Margaret plodded along going to this church or that. She knew she wasn't so good at religion. Her focus always was and would remain on being a decent and kind person.

Margaret would take a day off from school and take a bus fifty miles north from Mary Washington College in Fredericksburg to Washington, D.C. to visit with her father who she to that point did not consider herself to know. At the time, he worked on Wisconsin Avenue and she would spend the afternoon with him and go out to eat before returning to Mary Washington. Once she got a car, Margaret would drive into D.C., park by The National Mall, and taxi to her father's place. Dolly wasn't exactly happy about this, but Margaret had reached the age of making her own decisions. In time, Margaret grew to understand that her mother still loved her father and would until the day she died.

When Margaret graduated from college and moved to the area to begin teaching, she and her half-brother, JK, would spend the day together in D.C. roaming around the Smithsonian Museums and National Art Gallery, then taxi to the movies and dinner. JK would put three movies in a hat and Margaret would pick what to see. Margaret would put three restaurants in a hat and JK would pick where to eat. The following week, Margaret would put the three movies in, always foreign films, and JK would put the three restaurants in the hat and back and forth it went.

To this day, JK and Margaret both love foreign movies, art galleries, museums, and restaurants. To this day, they stream the same movies to watch like "Roma," a 2018 drama film shot in Mexico City. When JK and his partner, artist Margheith, came from their home in far-away Philippines to visit, they went first to the National Art Gallery in D.C.

Old Ebbitt Grill, the oldest bar and restaurant still open in Washington, remains their favorite. It began in the early 1800's in a hotel serving primarily members of Congress. In summers early on, hotels and restaurants would completely close when Congress adjourned. The restaurant finally became independent of the hotel, and well-known.

Margaret may have grown up in rural Virginia but she grew to love the city and taught JK to love the city. Their father might have been home drunk at times but they were each other's good companion and have remained so. This half-brother and half-sister developed by their own efforts their whole relationship.

JK, EVER SO IMPORTANT TO MARGARET, ONCE CHALLENGED his audience in a Toast Master's speech to reach out to a family member who they may have grown apart from. The speech began, "Once upon a time there lived a girl called Margaret Anne. Margaret Anne was born in 1935 in rural Virginia on the peninsula that forms the Chesapeake Bay which is called the Eastern Shore."

He described the isolation of this farming community and the closeness in what seemed to be about ten families related somehow by blood or marriage, and the nearby islands with their own English dialect. He described Margaret's mother staying and their mutual father moving for work first to Baltimore and then to Washington, D.C. JK finally learned he was not an only child. Margaret came into JK's world once she was in college.

Margaret moved to their Washington suburb upon graduating, he told his audience, and described how they bonded and tried their best to make up for the years "stolen from them" by their father. Jill who met Margaret in teaching became like a second sister extending a life-long commitment between Margaret and Jill to include important family like JK.

Through his words, JK expressed the enjoyment of his half-sister, her refusal to eat lamb after having pet lambs herself, her dislike of heights like crossing the Chesapeake Bay Bridge where she rewarded state police with boxes of cookies to drive her vehicle across. He would not leave out describing her voracious reading, guitar playing, photography, metal detecting, her love of Cuba and the study of the Spanish language. Of course, he would not leave out Margaret and Jill's king of the roost Maine Coon cat, Tristan.

JK concluded that they are closer than many siblings who did not have the separation forced on them. He ended his speech with an appeal. When families split apart, through hard work, nurture the love denied properly back in place as his love for Margaret and her love for him. JK now lives overseas and Margaret, being afraid of heights, will not travel by plane so they speak often by telephone. JK shares his closest thoughts and stories with the two people closest to him, his life partner, Marghieth, and Margaret Anne Savage.

IN THE 1950'S WHEN THERE WAS STILL PLENTY OF BEACH AT

Silver Beach, Margaret spent summers off from teaching at her family cottage visiting everyone back home. Her mother always insisted that Margaret be a part of her pranks. All year long, Margaret would look for hideous objects to buy at yard sales. They would carefully wrap them up and tag them to Mamie from Mrs. So-and-So who lived in town. Her aunt would feel bad not having given Mrs. So-and-So a gift in turn until she opened her gift, absolutely furious that someone would give her that sort of thing. Dolly loved playing tricks like this and was always ready for a good laugh.

Margaret brought friends to visit this wonderful place, water skiing all day, diving off the boat at night into the phosphorous loads in the bay water, coming up from the water looking like creatures from the famed Marvel films. Cooking out with bonfires ended their nights.

The early part of Margaret's teaching career, in summers, she and her Aunt Mamie ran the concession stand that Sanie and Nick had run before they passed away. Since Sunday was busy-busy, they fried huge pans of onions drawing people over for hot dogs, hamburgers, and softshell crab sandwiches. When the softshell crabs ran out, Margaret would run off on a hunt for more, bringing in more business. She made earning extra money seem as easy as she made teaching seem easy and no, it was not.

One Fourth of July, Aunt Mamie and Margaret were so absolutely busy in the stand, Dolly was relegated to cooking. Never being good at cooking, she muddled through preparing the hot dogs, hamburgers, and soft-shell crab sandwiches. Out of the blue after being gone several years, Jim Savage showed up and decided to take over like usual, decided they needed to make more money, and decided to drive the twenty miles to Chincoteague Island and buy one hundred and fifty dollars-worth of fireworks. Selling the fireworks, in turn, to the patrons brought five hundred dollars revenue in fireworks alone. Everything was fine until someone set a field on fire with the fireworks and the fire department had to come and knocked twenty-five dollars in fines off their earnings.

"That is just like Jim Savage to come in, take over, and cause mayhem," shrugged her mother. All three playing their roles, Margaret thought it was quite funny.

Making enough money that summer, the three ladies went on vacation. Margaret drove Dolly and Aunt Mamie to Miami in her red Volkswagen convertible and they had a blast. Dolly sat in the back with her legs hanging out so she could get a tan. Aunt Mamie and Margaret manned the front. This began an annual end-of-summer tradition, sometimes including cousin Hilda, memory-making that would cost all the summer's earnings and then some.

In later years, Dolly and Mamie had side-by-side homes after selling the farm and for years, watched soap operas talking about the people like they were relatives. After her sister passed away, Dolly never watched a soap opera again. She lived until the year 2004 dying at age ninety-four. Having always been a serious businesswoman, the week before she passed away, her words were, "Margaret Anne, I hope you are keeping my check book straight as I don't want any mistakes in it."

Silver Beach, to many, is more beautiful than even Key West. Vacationers still love it. Two of Margaret's dearest friends from high school, Eddie and Kirby, still live there. Old friend, Jackie Dewess, describes Silver Beach as the best place to raise a family, and to have a wonderful time.

The beach along the farm property and along the front row of cottages which was about twenty-five feet back from the Chesapeake Bay, now more than seventy-five years later, is gone due to erosion. The cottages on the waterfront have been relocated behind the third row of cottages, the second row at the waterfront, most now constructed with sea walls and docks. When Margaret and Jill visit or go to put flowers on the graves of her mother and grandparents, Margaret knows more people at the cemetery than alive on the Eastern Shore.

4
I JUST LOVED TEACHING

Originally, Margaret Savage was supposed to teach high school history and economics, neither available, she learned at the Fairfax County Public School teacher hiring fair. They offered her to teach government but government was about far too many rules, not Margaret's inclination, so she declined and exited. A man at the door overheard, grabbed her arm, and asked if she would consider teaching elementary school. Her answer, "I guess I can!" and that proved to be an understatement.

Thinking back on sixth grade, we were moving into our more social selves with our teacher being just the one to escort us through. I am certain we all felt that level of acceptance that Moggy felt in her own childhood. She brought the best of her own life growing up into our classroom.

Mrs. Wilkins was the principal of Layton Hall Elementary School and quickly regarded her new teacher as one of her own children. Of course, Margaret Anne gave her as many problems as any child could. Just wanting a day off of school, Margaret would in her most sickly voice call Mrs. Wilkins at home early in the morning telling Mr. Wilkins who answered the phone to let his wife know she needed a substitute that day. Mr. Wilkins would respond, "Moggy, get your ass into that school today!" to which she would reply, "Yes, sir."

Mr. and Mrs. Wilkins both had regard for and confidence in Miss Savage and when Mrs. Wilkins was out for the day, she would make the mistake of leaving Moggy in charge. Moggy would, in turn, pass a note around to her favorite teachers, "The cat is away."

Once when Mrs. Wilkins was preparing to paddle a student, she asked Margaret Savage to witness. Margaret Savage began a quiet laugh to which Mrs. Wilkins responded, "Margaret Savage! Am I going to have to paddle you, too?" Both Margaret Anne and the student escaped the paddle that day.

Each year when class assignments were handed to the teachers, Miss Savage's room was stacked full and some years with as many as 38 students. Mrs. Wilkins wanted her, yes her, to select which students to move to another class. Margaret wasn't going to do what she wasn't going to do and she was never going to do that. It broke her heart to lose a student.

After teaching a while and living with various people in a house and then an apartment, Margaret tired of the party life. By eleven-thirty at night, she was ready for sleep and that meant not fitting in anymore. Since she had continued to maintain contact with her father, she accepted his request to live with him and JK. The courts allowed JK to live full-time with their father after his third divorce if and only if the child's big sister moved in with them. She easily packed everything she owned into her 53 MG TD and took off for Rockville, Maryland.

The MG TD was produced by 1953. A 2-seater roadster combined an amazing drivetrain, a modified rear axle, the

MG Y-type chassis, a T-type style body, and an independent suspension on the front axle. The road-test report described the MG TD as transforming the comfort of riding. Dolly had told Margaret back in high school at the "ten cent store" she could one day leave The Shore, attend college, and afford her own sporty car and she did. This was the perfect car for Margaret Savage but not for long.

There was no Interstate 495 beltway around Washington, D.C. at the time, so the drive to her father's was straight through Georgetown, up Foxhall Road to get home to Rockville, Maryland across the Potomac River. Her father decided she needed a sensible car and traded that beautiful 53 MG TD for a Ford.

After a year of all this nonsense, they moved with their dog to Virginia into an apartment in Falls Church, closer to school. The apartment management discovered their huge Belgian Alsatian dog and gave them their moving papers. The dog had to go. Margaret cried having to let Sabra go though to a lively family with children to play with, a big house and a yard. Her father had none of the crying as the dog kept no secret of disliking him.

JK attended a different elementary school in Fairfax County than where Margaret taught. By the time they moved to Layton Hall Apartments around the corner from Layton Hall Elementary School, JK had missed the chance of having Miss Savage.

The secret kept on the Eastern Shore was that Dolly would come visit Margaret and her father and tell people she was going to visit her cousin in New Jersey. She must have trusted her sister because, at times, she brought Mamie along. Dolly developed a likeness for JK and once grown, JK would then go visit her. Once old enough to decide for himself, JK decided to go live with his own mother. He left in time to attend all of high school in Maryland. Margaret, as well, kept in contact with JK's mother and at some point, the third wife actually moved back in with her father, for a time. His handsome looks and charm only got him but so far.

JK grew up to serve in the Vietnam War stationed as a translator in Tokyo. He remained there taking several jobs overseas, playing rugby, and that is how he settled in Manila, Philippines. JK and dear Marghieth have two children, Kylie and Asti, JK's adopted daughter, Sonja, along with cats, a golden retriever, and not to forget the fish.

Their father passed away in 1976, the year we graduated from high school, most of us from Fairfax High School not far down the road from Layton Hall Elementary. He was never easy to deal with as Margaret learned best firsthand choosing to be in his life as an adult. He was a charmer and a mess at the same time. Margaret describes Jill as the kindest, brightest, most leveling person she has ever known. Without Jill's calm, she might have been like Jim Savage.

BACK IN THE 1960's, FAIRFAX CITY HAD TWO "RATTLE trap" shopping centers, one in each direction down a distance from our elementary school. One had the Safeway grocery store and the other had Bowl America bowling alley and Drug Fair. Once, my father bought me a fall which is a hair piece like a partial wig I saw behind the counter at Drug Fair. That place must have had everything. Both shopping strips had pizza parlors, we rode our bikes to without permission. I am not sure where we got the money but likely the change holder on dad's chest of drawers.

There were two low-rise medical arts buildings for the whole town, still in use today. Fairfax was far more populated than Silver Beach but not nearly as populated as today.

Tysons Corner Center, the "new climate-controlled, indoor mall" opened to the public in 1968. Fairfax Hospital opened in 1961 with 96 beds, today with more than ten times as many and a major trauma center. The Old Historic Courthouse now officially "historic" is replaced by a monstrous court complex including a massive detention center. Those locked up used to fit in a small brick annex just off the back of the old courthouse building with vertical iron bars feebly screwed in place. I drive by there today and still can't believe it.

Fairfax, now metropolitan, was a new suburbia when Margaret began her teaching career. Being a rural girl growing up surrounded by friendly, caring people she knew, this densely populated area we now live in can seem impersonal and unfriendly. Margaret fixes that by taking care of the people around her, lunch or afternoon cocktails for friends, cookies and kindness for those taking care of the lawn or working on her house, gestures of appreciation followed by hugs they steal from her. And she does not forget the store clerk. "I wish I could save the world," she says and this is nothing new. She would, one kindness at a time.

Life may have been more friendly back then but it was also more formal, and classrooms, too. We sat quietly in rows with minimal talking, without question. There was schoolwork to be completed and books were open. Miss Savage ventured comfortably away from that managing an amazing classroom balance of learning while seated and learning while up and about. She had control of her class without worrying about having control.

I remember having proper teacher supervision outside for recess but as we got older, I don't recall the class going out or coming in escorted by a teacher. We went and returned quietly. Hallways were that way. Besides, the older elementary students in our school got to be upstairs and that came with responsibility.

I remember so well and maybe we all do, our sixth grade teacher's blonde hair as if lightened by the sun on those summer days on the Chesapeake Bay. Thinking back now, I am not sure she even brushed it as I recall it to be short and natural, not poofy and coiffured which was the style back then. She and her classroom may have been less formal for back then but there was no mistaking, Miss Savage was the adult in the room with a talent for rapport with children. We just knew it, and we knew that the adult relationships throughout the halls of Layton Hall Elementary School worked because the school climate was unmistakably positive. I knew Miss Savage liked being there. Her good memories remain vivid.

Four activities that never happened twice, she would never forget. One year, she brought in her old ice cream freezer with the crank, salt and ice, and the ingredients to make ice cream outside the back door of the school. Thirty-three little sets of fingers set upon the paddle that came out with the frozen ice cream, a lot of laughter, and a mess everywhere. Second was the pinwheel peanut butter candy, unfortunately made indoors. Had someone in the class been allergic to peanuts, maybe this whole mess would not have happened.

They started with a tiny bit of mashed potatoes mixed with powdered sugar until doughy. They rolled it out, smeared on peanut butter, and then rolled it up tightly according to written directions and the challenge, with no spoken words. Of course, Miss Savage broke the silence with her laughter and felt bad for the poor people left to clean up after that dust storm.

The making of marzipan candy ended candy-making with

a story of all stories. Lots of dirty little hands combined all the ingredients into the shapes and colors of little fruit. How funny would it be to send the kid with the dirtiest hands to the most finicky teacher to sample the candy? Miss Savage told the student to make sure to stay until that generously shared piece of candy was eaten. Miss Savage laughed at the very thought of her clever prank and heard about it after school from the teacher on the receiving end. Of course, they all knew whose reputation for pranks always preceded her.

Tie dying shirts was the fourth and final bad idea she never repeated. Even with a sink in the room, tie dye went everywhere in this disaster of a project and heaven help the parents who might have washed those back-in-the-day popular shirts. Never again.

What did happen more than once was hatching chicken eggs in class. With a small hatchery, a plug-in heat source, and a dozen fertile eggs, the class was to open and examine one egg per week. Being big-hearted towards her students and towards the potential baby chicks, Miss Savage skipped that part and at least eight eggs managed to hatch by the end. One set of parents with a big family bravely allowed their son to bring home those chicks until one grew to be a rooster crowing at 5 AM in the morning. Time to be moved to a farm! A single mother from the same class shared a story about her son. He was going to hatch six eggs just as they had done in class. Miss Savage always loved the story about the little guy who put refrigerated eggs under his socks in the sock drawer.

When I approached her about hatching eggs in our class, her "yes" came easily. Three of us managed the project and felt fully responsible because Miss Savage taught that way. Miss Savage was involved and involved the whole class without taking it away from us. She again quietly bypassed weekly opening of the eggs. She was a smooth operator because everything in her class went smoothly and this project definitely did as my recollection remains as clear as hers.

I LEARNED ON SOCIAL MEDIA THAT BOBBY ROTHMAN ALSO had Miss Savage. We grew up across the street from each other on Country Hill Drive so share similar neighborhood memories. I did not know until now that we share similar sixth grade memories. He had Miss Savage the year before I did which meant the year before I had any concept of what this meant. When I contacted Bobby, he said that Miss Savage was "teacher of the century," a compliment I shared with her. Margaret said she once got "teacher of the year" but was not sure how. I told her the teachers who get that award without being sure how are the authentic ones and if Margaret Savage is anything, she is authentic.

Bobby messaged me a memory of Miss Savage drawing cartoon characters and pasting students' faces on them. The one she drew for him and he has kept in a box is *Pogo*, a kind-natured swamp possum from a long-running comic strip by cartoonist Walt Kelly. Bobby remembers this comic strip was from Miss Savage's childhood and a quick search shows Pogo was created in 1941. As Bobby describes, "Miss Savage really made you feel special."

Lisa Henry and I graduated together from Fairfax High School, both became teachers, retired, and recently during the summer met Margaret and Jill for cocktails in one of the outdoor "jungles" at Seacrets in Ocean City. My son could not believe my sixth grade teacher took us to Seacrets, a wild outdoor bar and restaurant on the water, with floating tables and chairs for swimsuit wearers. Margaret promised to take us to an older person bar next time and truth be told, we escaped the madness by going in the afternoon. I could not believe all of the "do you remembers" and successful "did you knows" between Lisa and Margaret. It reminded me how fortunate we were to live where we did, in "a small town" in a big city.

Margaret knew Lisa's mother who worked in our school cafeteria but more so, she knew Lisa's mother because Lisa's younger brother, Patrick, was in Miss Savage's class. Patrick was one of those active boys whose landing in Miss Savage's class was no accident. To this day, he is adventuresome, not to Miss Savage's surprise.

Lisa was and still is a natural performer which, by the way, makes her a peak performing grandmother. What I am saying is she has always been entertaining and never too serious. In school, it kept her on the edge of getting in trouble but then not because there was plenty of room for fun when we were coming along. At one point, she thought maybe she did not get into Miss Savage's class because she was not one of the cool kids who all seemed to be in Miss Savage's class. I would have been an outlier and so would Lisa because she was beyond fun and I was way serious, so cool and not cool.

With three younger brothers, Lisa was drawn back to Layton Hall Elementary. When Patrick was in sixth grade, Lisa had taken up ventriloquism with a Charlie McCarthy doll and would switch back on occasion from being a local college student to practicing her performances in her brother's classroom. And once, she brought stilts to their class. I am thinking there must have been other props and performances not mentioned. This was so very "Lisa" to even think of going and so very "Miss Savage" to even think of allowing her. This is so very "me" to love this story because it helps

make the case that Miss Savage was a very cool teacher,
indeed.

MARGARET GREW UP IN TIME TO ATTEND FOLK FESTIVALS LIKE
in Newport, Rhode Island and Paoli, Pennsylvania. It is so.
The envy of anyone who would stop and think, Margaret was
smart enough to go and not only listen to but chat with Joan
Baez, Pete Seeger, Joni Mitchell, Doc Watson, and others.
One favorite was a self-taught guitarist whose guitar has been
placed in the Smithsonian Museum. This left-handed player
played a right-handed guitar upside down, the melody with
her thumb and bass lines with her fingers. Elizabeth "Libba"
Cotten was black, born in North Carolina in 1893, not to priv-
ilege. She lived nearly 100 years and Margaret felt privileged
to have met her and heard her play.

Jill herself was not only an elementary school music
teacher but also an accomplished piano player. Margaret's
favorites were Debussy and Chopin played by Jill. They both
love opera and have seen the Metropolitan Opera and New
York City Opera at Wolf Trap National Park for the
Performing Arts known simply as "Wolf Trap." This one-
hundred-acre farm was donated to the National Park Service
in 1966 to become a large sheltered outdoor performance
venue in Northern Virginia.

Margaret played her own guitar at school some years but
not confidently, she says, limiting herself to a few chords. She
must have put her guitar down our school year. I would
remember. After teaching and a ten-year stint in real estate,
she picked up the guitar again and began playing notes, *Sola-
mente Una Vez* being her favorite song from age seven. This
romantic song, "You belong to my heart" was known also
from an old Gene Autry movie of the late 1940's. Margaret's

favorite renditions were played for her in a bar in Havana, Cuba and another time at a Russian hotel in Cienfuegos, Cuba. Her love of the music and of the Cuban people has always kept hold of her heart.

Opera, classical, and jazz music, no hard rock, and some blue grass and country music, especially the old style without electric instruments, have always been a part of her life. Emmy Lou Harris singing "Pancho & Lefty" hits a high note for Margaret, and Joan Baez singing "Manha de Carnaval." She loves traveling south and appreciates the Spanish language though "Manha de Carnaval" originates in Brazil in Portuguese.

Margaret and Jill do not travel without music in the car, first tapes, next quite a collection of compact discs, and then zip drives. Times are always changing though the love of music does not. Easy to lose a zip drive, impossible to lose a love of music.

The Beatles are more appreciated now than back in the day. Chet Baker always was and always will be appreciated. He was a jazz trumpet player and vocalist who caught the listening ear in the 1950's. Talking with Margaret about music is quite a lesson which means all these years later, I am still learning from her and as back in the day, learning from her is still an enjoyment. Recently vacationing on my friend's back deck overlooking the expansive Rideau River in Ottawa, Canada combined with the sounds of Chet Baker as recommended by Margaret Savage was just what the mental health specialist would have ordered.

There is a long list of music not so recognized by some of us these days that Margaret loves... Puccini, Nessun Dorma from Turandot, Liebestod from Tristan and Isolde, Bachianas Brasileiras by Villa-Lobos and currently, Adele. This may be more of a testament to her sharp mind at the age of eighty-five or a putting to shame of the rest of us for not knowing these musical talents. Some looking into this by the rest of us may be in order. May our minds be as clear thirty years after retirement as our beloved teacher's. I teasingly told her as we worked on this project, if her mind starts to slip, start writing fast! I don't see that happening.

I REMEMBER MISS SAVAGE ALWAYS SMILING. SHE SMILED AT the class and she smiled at each one of us individually and the message of the importance of each student was clear. Miss Savage's light and loving heart towards others was perfect for me but also for everyone else she ever had or would have in class. She enjoyed all those many complex little beings who came to her with their own uniquenesses.

One time, Miss Savage brought a friend to school for the whole day. I must have created a one-person welcoming committee because I remember inviting him into class activities and sitting beside him on the hillside at recess. He later wrote me a thank you letter which was a very good idea. He must have been a lot like Miss Savage teaching children to feel good about the nice things they do.

Miss Savage selected me to narrate our school play that year, "A Christmas Carol." I vividly remember getting on and off the stage between acts and each time, her stooping down smiling telling me I was doing a wonderful job. Her sincerity with children brought the sense of confidence we needed in those moments. Knowing her today, I see the same appreciation for others, and support. I jokingly told her when we first started talking about writing her story, "Besides, I need to do something to thank you for selecting me to narrate the sixth grade play."

That year for the first time, I got straight A's. A quiet girl

in class had stayed back at recess to help Miss Savage set up some sort of project in the back of the room and at the last minute, I stayed back to help. Why Kathy mentioned getting straight A's, I do not remember but this one classmate making this one comment triggered a big shift. I hadn't been concerned with academics, studying for spelling tests just before going to bed the night before. At that moment, I knew I would start getting straight A's.

Miss Savage never worried about grades when she was a student, or tried to out-compete others, never felt the need to prove herself to anyone, or to become something she was not, I find out now. That may well have set the tone for my endeavor back then. I just wanted to get good grades and did with an occasional slip, not to worry. Miss Savage taught us not to worry. Still, back then, I was the constant on-looker. My facial expression must have been too pensive from grade school on up. I was always the observer at the party who would rather be home writing about the party even though I didn't know it.

Peter Greaves was a different story. He was "the party." Of course, I remember how Peter stood in sixth grade, one foot cocked inward atop the other, seemingly double-jointed, knees tucked up against each other tilted towards a classmate's desk. He seemed dexterous and nimble both physically and socially. My daughter's teacher in third grade once said, "itch that she is," and Peter was definitely "an itch" handled well by Miss Savage.

Peter was always up and all over the place. He was in there not to observe his classmates, he was in there to socialize and he did. He had the cutest mannerisms and the cutest of cute face. I think his baseline was a natural smile like Miss Savage's was. He seemed happy there and comfortable and okay with Miss Savage addressing him to sit back down. And then he was up and about again.

I look back now and would call him a networker. I imagine him today as successful, harnessing those good social skills, that clear desire to get up and go, and the charm that made him so clearly liked by his classmates. I do see Peter today on social media and honoring his mother who passed away. At the same time, I am talking to Margaret Savage who also taught Peter's sister, also talking about how lovely their mother was. Though Peter's family moved to Texas sometime after that year, he remains to this day friends with Miss Savage and she to this day loves Peter.

Layton Hall Elementary drew from four or five surrounding neighborhoods and besides not keeping up socially with Peter and his friends, I walked home in a different direction to a different neighborhood. Most of us lived in single-family homes with those small yards to play in and streets to run around on. On weekends and in summers, we were free to roam as long as we checked in with home at key times like lunch and dinner and were allowed to play outside after dark. Flashlight tag was most fun and the big boys who seemed so big in upper elementary grades when we were in lower elementary grades would on occasion stir up pranks.

I hesitated to tell Margaret about one of their childhood pranks back then but she accepted it as it was. Margaret, I am sure knowing her now twice in my life, accepts what is or can't be changed and impacts what can be through her own efforts, with kindness, and encouraging others to do the same. So one day one summer, the big boys organized us all to ride our bikes to Layton Hall Elementary nearly a mile away. Not needing parental permission to wander, we went. They had planned without telling the rest of us one boy would be "it."

When we got to the school, they announced "bicycle hide-and-seek" and told the one boy to hide at the blacktop around the side of the back corner of our dark red brick school building and count to one hundred. We were supposed to hide with our bikes in the woods back behind the school as there was a tract of woods with paths and a stream called Daniels Run. The big boys instead had us all sneak and ride home.

We resumed playing on our street and the boy who was "it" came around the corner what seemed like a long time later. He walked his bike down to his house, dropped it in his yard, and slump shouldered, went inside. Thankfully, I was not part of planning this prank which was clever and still hits my funny bone yet may have gone too far. At some time, each of us might have found ourselves on the wrong side of a prank we took in stride.

Moggy had her own "head-on-home" prank. Snipes are birds that live on the shore and in marshlands but avoid dense vegetation. They are neither tame nor friendly. Snipes have long slender, sharp-pointed bills and will use them. When city kids visited the farm, Moggy told them snipes are tame and friendly and sent them out in the fields with sacks to catch snipes. The city kids would wander a long way down to beat the bushes to scare out the snipes that really did not exist there. No snipe would ever end up in a sack and while the city kids were taking hours to figure all this out, Margaret and company were long since back home.

A MOST FOND RECOLLECTION AT OUR ELEMENTARY SCHOOL was recess across that wide-open field out back where pick-up softball took place and that's exactly where one of my "picked on" moments took place. We organized ourselves. I

am absolutely certain Miss Savage never organized us at
recess and never had need to intervene in our free play. The
role our teachers played was allowing us enough time to both
organize and play the game to some level of satisfaction
before settling back, red-faced, sweaty, winded, and mentally
available again for learning in the confines of a classroom.
We came straight in and settled down quickly because not
"listening to and following directions" would not please our
parents. Nothing was the teacher's fault in those days.

I remember being picked last in sixth grade at one of
those pick-up softball games at recess where a couple of the
kids scoffed in disappointment. When my time came to bat,
bases were loaded and I cracked that softball out of the "ball
park" bringing in four runs just before the teacher blew the
whistle for us to come in. Those kids gawked in disbelief.
That was a confidence builder anyone at that age could use.

Being always the observer, I noticed one of the more
socially confident classmates brought to school a thick
rubber-banded stack of index cards, one for each book she
had read, each with details of each book. Besides being
impressed, I realized this most outgoing person I went to
school with must have carved out plenty of alone time to
read. That fascinated me at the age when differences in
people became more apparent and cliques were beginning to
form.

We had a way of meeting social challenges. Teachers got
involved when needed but they did not manage our
exchanges and I'm thankful for that. Miss Savage put trust in
us to find our way though she was well aware and fostered
the positive. She had learned herself to successfully navigate
the academic and social challenges of school and knew we
could, too. Her level of awareness came naturally, throughout
her childhood, through her teaching years, and today

evidenced by all the lives she has impacted and all the positive, lasting relationships enriching her life. This is not to say she was able to avoid life's travails but rather she managed them and always came back to the good.

Not being protected from simple social travails teaches us how to cope in life, and to be empathetic. I don't remember being picked last again my whole childhood but it was more like those few minutes between being picked last and hitting that home run were enough for me to learn that I could survive being "picked last." I remain ever more sensitive to anyone "picked last."

School was for learning to "get along well with others," an important area on the report card but mostly, school was about reading, writing, arithmetic, and by sixth grade, science and history. Learning had begun feeling like trudgery which implies moving forward as if in mud. I should take responsibility for this though the feeling lifted in Miss Savage's class. She was a show, don't tell role model. How did Miss Savage do it? I just know she did.

Moggy surely engaged in more antics and pranks than usual in her day and she clearly did not buy into what seemed meaningless to her. Her description of early years in school may have been drudgery which is associated with menial or dull work. Miss Savage must have gotten down to what was important in the content of our sixth grade class because it was neither trudgery nor drudgery. Her light-hearted ability to tease and have fun from early on showed up for us as ease and comfort in Miss Savage's classroom no matter what we were learning.

We also had gym class playing crab soccer in the cafeteria, feet out front, hands down low and stretched behind holding us up off the tables-pushed-back, just-cleaned floor. The dress code required girls to wear dresses or skirts so on gym day, we wore gym shorts underneath the whole garb. Tennis shoes came to school in backpacks and were allowed only during play. "School shoes" were required outside of gym class and "school clothes" came off after school in exchange for "play clothes." And then there were "Sunday clothes" that Margaret had to wear on Sundays growing up, too. Those days of "Sunday best" are not altogether gone but close.

No matter where she was or how she had to dress, Margaret did not much care for formality and structure so she not only disliked gym class for herself growing up, but for us, as well. She preferred us running free at recess over gym class. And she loved Art. Mary Hope Stowers Worley, one of Margaret's principals at Layton Hall Elementary, became an artist after retirement displaying her works in shows. She claimed her love of art was Margaret's fault.

Of course, Margaret would not like those formal observations as part of the teacher evaluations. When Mary Hope would ask her what she would be teaching at ten AM on a particular day, Margaret would say, "Art."

"What about twelve-thirty?"

"Art."

"Two o'clock?"

"Art."

Margaret would tell her to please come whenever she wanted to see whatever she wanted because nothing would change with parents in the room, guests, or principals doing teacher evaluations. The quality of her life experiences, the person she was, lead to an assured ability to handle her class. And her ability to handle any "wild child," having been one herself, would not falter. Just being herself teaching us to be ourselves in itself deserved a strong evaluation. I do hope that has not been forgotten by those evaluating teachers all these years later. If so, smuggling a bit of Margaret into any school program today is advisable.

I am surprised by how many people from our elementary days still remain in contact with each other, even those who moved away getting together with others who moved away or scattered friends finding their way back to each other when the opportunities arise. The memory-making lives on.

Growing up in a rural area, Margaret may not have had lots of children to run out her front door to play with but as we can tell, they managed to create plenty of their own memory-making . Children in the 1940's growing up in her time and children in the 1960's growing up in our time were simply not closely supervised. The out of doors was considered safe and roaming free felt good and made room for a lot of learning outside the classroom.

Our street being just shy of one mile from the school did not qualify us to ride the bus so we walked. The lane at school for parents to drop their kids off and pick them up was not invented yet but yellow rain slickers and rubber shoe covers known as goulashes were. We walked, rain or shine.

Fairfax County experiences summer temperatures in the nineties and below freezing temperatures in the winter with three or four annual snowfalls. With poor weather forecasting back then, we would wake up to a foot of snow on the ground and surprise school closings. In our suburban neighborhoods on "snow days," the kids were out building igloos and snowmen in our front yards, having snowball fights and sledding, coming back indoors for breaks to thaw out and warm up. I'm glad now that Miss Savage got those snow days off from school, too, a gift of time she deserved and had not experienced growing up.

Northampton County where Margaret grew up is warm
and muggy in the summer reaching the mid-80's with few if
any days below freezing and nearly no snow in the winter
largely due to the close proximity to water. Though she grew
up in that rural setting, Miss Savage embraced and enjoyed
our suburban one which became hers, too. She enjoyed not
only her students and the families she got to know, she
enjoyed our easy access to everything in Washington, D.C.
and the many friends she made and kept over the years
through teaching.

Much more was going on at Layton Hall Elementary than
any sixth grader could have imagined. Mrs. Schwartz taught
third grade and was kind, reminding Margaret of how her
own third grade teacher, Mrs. Henry, had been kind. Once,
Mrs. Schwartz's husband was in Walter Reed Army Hospital,
at the time located on the far side of Washington. No one
wanted to make the drive so Margaret volunteered to drive
her to see him. Having never driven past the National Mall
just inside D.C. nearest to Virginia, she would normally drive
to The Mall, park her car, and flag a taxi to restaurants and
theaters.

This time, she picked Mrs. Schwartz up in her tiny 53
MG TD sports car, top down, and drove her not only to
Walter Reed Hospital but also to a shoe store who knows
where along the way in a part of Washington never to be seen
again. Mrs. Schwartz bought her fancy shoes and arrived in
fashion at Walter Reed to see her husband nearly an hour and
a half later, Miss Savage winding her way around this way
and that to get there. They arrived home before dark and Mrs.
Schwartz hesitated to ask for a ride again as did anyone else.
News spread fast.

Our principal, Mrs. Wilkins, seemed old and serious,
running the school well. Seeming unhumored may have been

the key to her success. We would not have known how fun Miss Savage's relationship with her was. Mysteriously, Miss Savage was always put in charge of the faculty gift committee. This always insured Mrs. Wilkins getting her gift of choice. They shared a wonderful wit and humor.

Once during a faculty meeting, one of the Fairfax County Public School supervisors attended. Mrs. Flapin was known to put fear into most and everyone was scared to say a word. During the meeting, Miss Savage openly disagreed with her and Mrs. Wilkins nearly died that moment. At the end of the meeting, Mrs. Flapin put her arm around Miss Savage and asked her what she was doing that evening. She and Jill were going to Wolf Trap to see the Metropolitan Opera.

Mrs. Edna Flapin invited herself to join them getting a last-minute ticket from a parent of a student of Miss Savage's who managed Wolf Trap at the time. One worry was their casual lawn seating located behind the more formal seating to the front and another worry was having drinks in front of Mrs. Flapin. Miss Savage has always enjoyed martinis and Jill champagne. Mrs. Flapin brought champagne and strawberries and was not, after all, someone to fear at faculty meetings.

Mrs. Flapin was the connection for Peter being in our class. I was in there because of a lucky draw. Peter was in there because somebody smart and thoughtful knew Miss Savage was just the right teacher for him.

Mrs. Wilkins was kind through the years visiting Margaret at her mother's beach cottage at Silver Beach. Mr. Wilkins would steer the boat as Margaret showed off her waterskiing abilities. You could take the girl out of Silver Beach but you could not take Silver Beach out of the girl.

When Mrs. Wilkins retired, her portrait remained on the wall. In later years, Layton Hall got a principal who would

take down Mrs. Wilkin's portrait and Miss Savage made it
her business to put it back in place until it came down again,
then back in place again. Miss Savage finally tired of playing
"Antigone," the Greek mythical daughter of Oedipus,
"worthy of one's parents." Memories of Mrs. Wilkins and
stories about their time together lived on without need of the
portrait.

MARGARET SAVAGE TAUGHT TWENTY-EIGHT YEARS AT
Layton Hall Elementary School starting with her wonderful
principal, Mrs. Wilkins. Mary Hope Worley, who followed,
loved a good joke as Margaret Anne Savage did. A good
sense of humor with a touch of devilment diffuses many a
situation creating a positive school and a positive classroom
environment as we were so fortunate to be in.

Once a student unraveled a knitted sweater in class, tied a
weight to the end, and lowered it out the second story
window. Miss Savage hurried to the office downstairs to
inform Mrs. Worley who went outside, tied a note to the
dangling end, and gave the wool thread a good tug. Mean-
while, Miss Savage and Mrs. Worley went back upstairs to
greet this inventive and mischievous student as he reeled it in.
They all three got a good laugh. Let's hope that sweater had
not been hand knit by a loving mother.

Mary Hope became a close friend and Margaret hated to
see her go. Jim Tiernan replaced her and he was kind, as well.
And then, he left. By 1985, Miss Savage's run with Layton
Hall came to an end as she transferred to neighboring West-
more Elementary and retired in 1990. Years prior, Zellwood
Ferguson took the transfer to John C. Wood Elementary
directly across the highway, and likely to allow Margaret
Savage to remain in her beloved sixth grade classroom at

Layton Hall. Zell was a wonderful role model and like Mama, always said what was good, followed by tactful suggestions. Zell had quite an impact on Margaret's life, never to be forgotten. They remained in contact until she passed away years later.

Many relationships that began so well have lasted. Mrs. Renfrow who taught me in third grade had a stroke and moved in with her daughter and son-in-law. She still recognizes Miss Savage. Mrs. Garwood and Miss Savage, who joined the Layton Hall faculty the same year, speak often and meet for lunch on occasion still laughing about Mrs. Garwood being the lone soul willing to adventure regularly in Margaret's MG convertible. They traveled on backroads, often over to Great Falls Park at the Potomac River, a beautiful rocky area that separates Maryland from Virginia, and downtown into Washington, D.C. to the movies. Though the sporty little MG was traded in for a not-so-sporty Ford, a red Volkswagon convertible and a sweet little Karmann Ghia were in Margaret's future.

Mrs. Margaret Johnson also taught sixth grade, two Margarets directly across the hall from each other. Teddy got moved into her class from Miss Savage's class, as mentioned earlier, and my own brother had Mrs. Johnson. Both loved her. Once, she and her husband and son came to our house for dinner to thank her for being a wonderful teacher. Miss Savage proudly wore clothes given her by Mrs. Johnson as she needed them and though handed along, they were so very fine.

Her son, Alec, who was "get-in-line cute" sparked my first crush. He made it into Miss Savage's sixth grade class a year ahead of me, unfortunately. He was as kind and gentle as his mother, serious about important things, yet able to laugh just as his mother. They became Margaret and Jill's neighbors outside the school building, as well, in a townhouse development a few miles away. In a letter dated July 2008 after the passing of Margaret Johnson, Margaret Savage wrote to Lloyd and Alec of wonderful memories and thank-yous, beginning with appreciation for the encouragement to purchase their beloved Ocean City vacation property.

At the time, they were all staying at the well-known Phillips Hotel. Lloyd threatened to buy this townhouse if Margaret and Jill did not so they did. Lloyd also got Margaret into her long-standing love of metal detecting and what better place to begin than along the beach? "Treasure" means first the best treasure found, that of a treasured friendship.

Lloyd allowed Margaret to go out by herself on his Zodiac boat and ever after, when she sees one, she thinks of those good times. The memories do not end without the mention of mixing drinks for breakfast in Atlantic City, turning green on gambling boats in Florida and not from gambling, enjoying fireworks on those Fourth of Julys aboard Captain Lloyd's boat, and Lloyd swiping a coffee mug from the Annapolis Yacht Club. From parties in the city with big paper lanterns filled with sand and lit candles to weekends on a farm with snakes that kept down the mosquitoes, there is no measure of this friendship. The memories and love that drift through their minds, never forgotten, signed with love, "Moggy and Jill."

Along with harmonious relationships with fellow teachers, Margaret remained always comfortable with parents. All of the parents over all of the years were welcome to freely visit her classroom without restriction, with always a job for them to step into such as giving attention to a little person or listening to one read. One day per year was designated as a parent visitation day, a big production as the teachers and administrators did care. Teachers did not look forward to that day but it never bothered Miss Savage because as in any other school day, there were no secrets, there was no show. That day was like each of the other days except more bodies in a usually crowded classroom.

Margaret used up all of her sick days over those years. Perhaps those mental health "sick days" saw her through. She would maybe go to the beach or to a movie, or stay home and read. Sometimes she spent time helping her father with his issues later in life. Why she was not at school remained her own personal reasons. With a five dollar pay out from the school system for each remaining sick day upon retirement, she did not draw any attention to the two dollar and fifty cents she was due for that remaining one half of one sick day. Anyone would conclude that she used those days well as the days in school were magnificent as all of us whose lives she touched can attest. Margaret's states simply, "I just loved teaching."

5

A LORELEI CALLING

Upon retiring after thirty-three years with an average of thirty-three students per year, over a thousand students had crossed her classroom threshold more than six thousand mornings. That is over two hundred thousand times students crossed through that happy doorway, one student at a time, and one teacher, into a classroom we shared together, would always remember and never forget.

After teaching, working at Blockbusters video rental store became an endeavor to get first dibs on videos to bring home to watch. That didn't work out so well. She considered working in hardware at Home Depot, after all, everyone working at Home Depot knew exactly where everything was. Margaret never knew where a damn thing in that store was. They were wondering why with her particular qualifications, she would seek employment there. And so she did not.

What Margaret did do was enter the people business still. She and Jill decided to move from their townhouse to a house with a yard in a sweet nearby town in Fairfax County known as Clifton. Acquiring a magnolia tree that dropped leaves needing sweeping up was a bonus. Margaret, thus, caught sight of the real estate business. As with her respect for and wonderful relationships with principals, so she had with the broker, Frank Lee, of Long and Foster on Prosperity Avenue. None of the other six companies on the other six avenues she visited had quite the epitome of broker professionalism and kindness so she joined with Frank's office and remained for ten years. Frank and Marge Lee and their entire family were not only dear friends but became next door neighbors in the townhouse in Ocean City.

Any student such as I who knew her in the kid world would not want to share Miss Savage with the any other world except, this move into real estate was one of her better moves in life. What was good for our teacher would be okay with any of us. Her love of people and enjoyment in helping them make honest and smart home investments left her able, each night, to put her head on the pillow and sleep peacefully. I imagine she slept peacefully as a teacher, too. Real estate, like teaching, like her childhood on the Eastern Shore, brought Margaret Savage so much good and the best of friends.

THE BIKE MAY BE STATIONARY THESE DAYS BUT THE COUPLE of miles of treasure hunting was not. The morning treks metal detecting spanned over fifty years of a hobby involving more than a few metal detectors. The first metal detector from an Army Navy Surplus store came with a giant battery pack and a giant battery pack seemed to attract giant thunderstorms and certainly would attract lightening which often meant not getting out of there fast enough.

Enjoying the hobby long enough meant experiencing metal detector improvements so a Whites was followed by a

Minelab and Fisher metal detector, always seeking the best
available. Just as in teaching, the person we knew as "Miss
Savage" who gained pleasure in helping us and making us
feel happy helped vacationers find lost valuables making
them feel happy. Spending the summers by the ocean meant
developing a following, Margaret's metal detector groupies.

One favorite was a gentleman whose wife had lost an
earring. Their son was six years old at the time and even
when the son was in college, this dad came over to Margaret
at the beach each year to thank her again for finding his
wife's anniversary present. Many pieces of jewelry and a lot
of money never reunited with their owners and sit quietly in
Margaret's safe deposit box. Not everything found was of
value but finding certain things did have value. Finding over
five hundred fish hooks spared a lot of potential feet. A share
of tent pegs reunited with Scout masters, and trash collected
along the way did not make its way into the ocean.

A glimpse into this hobby uncovered unfavorite stories
such as people losing wallets and phones which meant
Margaret thoughtfully contacting them only for them to ask
her to bring their found possessions to them, not offering to
come to her. Even as a sixth grader, I would have known our
teacher not to be a pushover and correctly. In reply, she
always declined but offered to bury it back where she found it
and disclose to them the location.

Believe it or not, metal detecting can be hurtful to
someone who chooses in life never to be hurtful. Once upon
finding a young lady's eleven thousand dollar ring and
declining payment for the find, Margaret asked that she
donate to the Worcester County Animal Society. As this
young lady walked away with that beautiful ring reunited
with her finger, she stated that because it was insured, she
was not going to tell her husband. She never did donate to the

animal shelter where Margaret regularly donates, a no-kill shelter always in need.

Such a world, Margaret could never be a part of and did not enjoy witnessing. People began staking out their own little territories on the beach, not to be crossed, which caused an occasional remark about who was really paying the taxes for that beach territory meaning Margaret whose beach property came with a tax. People also stopped wearing jewelry on the beach and began using "plastic" rather than "loose change" which ended this end of the hobby.

The Fisher CZ 21 metal detector still finds treasures every once in a while, because all people who metal detect are dreamers and treasure hunters. These pirates who love the hobby, love the dream and share that love. A respect and admiration passes down to new treasure hunters. Margaret always tied a pirate scarf around her head while treasure hunting. Those who laughed only thought they had grown up. They did not understand that those who in some ways never grow up, at least in their own minds, love life as Margaret, respected and admired, dreamer and treasure hunter.

FROM EARLY VACATIONS BY CAR TO FLORIDA TO LATER vacations by cruise ship, Margaret and Jill have never hesitated to travel. The three "People to People" cruises to Cuba stand above any other. How would Margaret begin to write about her travels to Cuba? Would she approach it from dreams of being a child of a wealthy sugar plantation owner back in the 1940's and 50's or as a child of a slave working for that same plantation owner? Would she have had the same dreams, the same wishes? Yes, because she would have wished for food and water, music and people around her, and love. Both of those children would have, though the first would have more abundant food.

Perhaps they would have had fear, the fear of the plantation owner by the slave child and the fear of what could happen by the plantation owner's child. Margaret was neither of those children as an eighteen year old in 1953 when she was invited to go with a friend to Cuba aboard his parent's yacht. She simply could not go because Mama was ill. Had she gone, she would have seen one side of Cuba, that of the wealthy plantation owner and of the Mafia who controlled the gambling, prostitution, and nightlife of a Cuba known only to those of affluence.

Many years passed between 1953 and when no Americans could visit Cuba until a recent window, now shut. When Margaret could go, she did go, a Lorelei calling her. The Lorelei, a high and steep slate rock formation on the bank of the River Rhine in Germany, full of folklore and modern myth inspiring tales of enchantment and betrayal, did not call even to her imagination while there as Cuba has. She has also visited Mexico, and Spain, and Puerto Rico. None called her as the people of Cuba, full of spirit and love, and hope. Margaret stood at the front of the cruise ship as it entered the harbor of Havana, barren of small boats unlike any harbor ever to visit.

The terminal, one of three, was the only one with a roof. Customs was formidable, stepping into one of seven enclosures. The person behind the desk requested the removal of all outer garments and glasses. Baggage was scanned through a conveyor machine. After a look up and down, stamping the passport, and taking the visa, visitors were then free to go.

Money was exchanged next at the bank, US dollars for CUC, the Cuban Convertible Peso used by travelers and pinned to the US dollar. The CUP, the national currency used by local Cubans, on the other hand, is the peso with pictures of famous people like the revolutionary Che on the two-peso CUP. The CUC is the peso with pictures of famous buildings for which Margaret's one hundred dollars exchanged for eighty-seven CUC. She was ashamed at the bank and apologized to the teller for an ungentlemanly man screaming at the teller over the exchange rate which could be as much as one dollar to one CUC. But really?

From the bank, the way down was by elevator or the forty-five steps to street level to meet the Chinese manufactured tour buses, comfortable enough and with restrooms in the rear. The architecture of Cuba is varied, magical and splendid, the opera house, beautiful. Though many buildings were in disrepair, many were in the midst of repair. The Cubans were rebuilding as best they could. Their capitol building, a copy of the capitol building in Washington, DC, stands proudly two inches taller. Photos were allowed.

Across the harbor stands a statue of Christ, "Cristo de la Habana," rising to a height of two hundred and fifty-nine feet with a sweeping view of Havana. A gift from the wife of an early leader, Batista, likely a Christian woman trying to make up for the sins all around her. Batista played footsie with the Mafia from the 1940's up into the 60's, lived at one time in Daytona Beach, and donated art to a museum there as he was said to have stolen art from the Cuban people. They want their art back. They did not want the fall of Cuba to communism, according to the book, *Havana Nocturne*, by T.J. English.

The Cuban people love to say Christ, in the statue, is holding a box of cigars and a bottle of rum. The people of Cuba are really wonderful and resilient. Margaret was pulled back to her youth growing up on the Eastern Shore, the friendliness and helpfulness of the people, what she now in her later years misses in today's world. Where has all the kindness gone? The people of Cuba, their love and kindness, are the siren's call.

The Cuban people do not have things. They have love and kindness in lieu of things. They travel about safely in Havana with the threat only from the cubes of ice in their drinking water. Swallow down quickly, travelers are told. And at life's end, the Cuban people need only a few dollars for a burial in a beautiful cemetery. Ongoing since the 1930's, even one evening in the Tropicana nightclub means love. The club is outdoors with at least one hundred dancers and singers in wonderful costumes, Cuban entertainers weaving the magician's spell.

Making do with what they have, the Cuban people keep cars for years and years. Most noticeable on the streets are these wonderful American cars from the 1950's. Painted in absolutely fantastic colors, turquoise, purple, bright orange, and deep yellow, more beautiful than any of the original colors of the 1950's and the fact that these cars are still going strong seventy-plus years later is symbolic of the very nature of the Cuban people. Throughout the countryside are these cars still being painted and worked on, held together with everything that can possibly work. Walk by any car owner along the street and they happily lift the hood for any man, woman, or child and explain the engine of an American 1950's car.

In our world where cars are easily traded in every five years, could the workmanship from well over a half a century ago have been better? Not likely. The Lada, a Russian car, sometimes shows up on the street in Cuba, as well, though the saying goes, "Yeah, Lada. They are a Lada trouble."

After three visits to Cuba, Margaret was saddened by the news that the United States government once again closed off travel there. These wonderful, welcoming people would not hurt anyone. In sight for them was finally the opportunity to make money driving people around, selling them tickets, and rum of course, teaching them about their loving and kind ways. Passing the Malecon in Havana, the broad roadway and seawall along the coast, tears filled Margaret's eyes as the people called, "Come back! We love you!"

Her dream came true to visit Cuba, to go back in time to the Eastern Shore of decades gone by, not the architecture but the people, the siren's call. She would go again yet not tied to a mast with the beauty of the Cuban people out of reach.

WHILE FAMILY AND FARM SURROUNDED MARGARET AS A child, students and travel have surrounded her as an adult. Both friends and pets have surrounded her always. Being a girl from a farm who buried dead birds in funeral services in grandma's flower garden, Margaret notices birds in peril. In fact, she notices birds.

That coastal wetland she grew up in attracts the shorebird called the killdeer with a wingspan of twenty-five inches and a vivid black and white ringed neck. Margaret could not miss the beautiful contrast but she did miss sprinkling the tail with salt to acquire a pet as Mama had told her. The other bird prevalent in those agricultural fields is the Virginia quail known for its bird call, "bob-white." Smaller, with a wing-span of fifteen inches, the male is more colorful also with a vivid black and white color contrast at the neck. The killdeer is more visible but neither are catchable though one bird one day would end up so lucky.

Margaret's favorite bird of all is the willet and she did have a pet willet named Kiwi. Kiwi developed a bad leg and fortunate for Kiwi, it lived in Ocean City, Maryland with adult Margaret who with Jill drove it fifty-five miles to the Tristate Bird Rescue in Newark, Delaware. This bird bit everyone except Margaret. He snuggled with her, nestling in the bend of her arm gazing up at her sideways.

At age four, Margaret snuggled with her pet lamb named "Baby Lamb." At age sixty-five, her father named his dog, "Black Dog." This naming streak did crop up on occasion. And there was a dog in her life at one time named "Baby." "Midnight" was her cat as a child who loved to eat oysters and went with Margaret down on the boat to get them for Mama for dinner. Margaret thought cats simply appeared and never knew anyone would pay for a cat. Cats and oysters on the farm by the bay were free.

Margaret's Belgian Alsatian dog, Sabra, was a gift from a psychiatrist she dated for a couple of years. Did she first go see this psychiatrist? No. A friend wanted them to meet and when he arrived for the first time, wanting to make a good impression, she was sitting on the roof of the house she was renting.

While taking the psychiatrist to the airport one time, Margaret was approached by a policeman for parking in a "No Parking" zone. While parking in the "No Parking" zone might not have gotten her in trouble, her Belgian Alsatian dog jumping at the policeman through the convertible top did. The convertible top had to be replaced. The dog got her in more trouble but he got her out of trouble, too. Sabra was trained to disrupt chess board games on secret command if Margaret was losing.

Dolly never liked Sabra's poor behavior, dragging anyone holding the leash down the boat ramp. Sabra was not allowed in Dolly's house which created another problem. Not needing to be walked, cats were easier.

Max was one of a few rescue cats and a guttersnipe, he

was. When he went blind, there were few funds for veterinary care. When Jill found out the veterinary ophthalmologist's second practice was in New York City, they knew the only help for Max, the guttersnipe, was love.

The first cat purchased was a no-tail Manx. Margaret and Jill drove to Charleston, South Carolina to get him. Had they gotten the red-coated female, they would have named her Scarlett. They took the brother, Rhett, who was white and lived to age eighteen. Who would forget Scarlett and Rhett in the epic romance story, "Gone With the Wind?" Pet names were often based on classics of one sort or another.

As with the Manx breed, Rhett was friendly to them but hid from other people. They then had a lilac Siamese cat, given to them due to the owners being allergic. Mandy had one fault. In the day of fur coats, she would lick the fur coats of guests at the party if Margaret and Jill were not careful. Ludwig was a Maine Coon who came along on Beethoven's birthday and lived eighteen years. Outgoing, free-wheeling, and social, Maine Coons fit right in.

Tristan is the current cat. Tristan's name came from the favorite twelfth century tragic romance opera, *Tristan and Isolde*, by Wagner. Tristan has never seen it because Margaret and Jill won't take him to the opera. He would probably ignore the opera if he went and that would be a waste of time and money.

Jill is Tristan's mom and when I was visiting in what must have been a tired state, I asked if Tristan was a rescue cat. Tristan is a Maine Coon. Neither Jill nor Margaret flinched. I thought I noticed Tristan flinch and I did flinch on my way home, so embarrassed. Though they loved rescuing cats, Tristan is no rescue cat. After I left, I heard that Tristan asked what that lady was talking about.

Tristan is a very intelligent cat. He has three homes, the

one in Northern Virginia where I met him, one in Ocean City, Maryland, and one in Daytona Shores, Florida where Jill, Tristan, and Margaret were heading when I first met Tristan. The car rides on those road trips between residences are no problem. The Inca Indians could not do a better job packing the car so not a knife blade could get between things yet there is always room for Tristan.

No matter the assurances, he sometimes worries there may be no room and he may be left behind. The big high he gets from the catnip socks Jill gives him must help him over-look the possibility. Then again, when his dog harness goes on, he knows he's in. Being an only cat, what Tristan likely does not know is that he is a large cat, so no cat harness fits him. His size doesn't prevent him from sleeping on the bed at night with Jill and besides, the need to guard Jill is always present in his mind.

Tristan has a lot of emotional intelligence, too. He easily transitions from one home to the other, settles in nicely, and behaves as he wishes. He knows not to lay on a jigsaw puzzle until it is complete and loves resting in the puzzle box top. He will perform acrobatic acts to jingle chandelier crystals. He must be practicing reaching way high upward on hind legs for when spaghetti noodles are held above him. He wouldn't miss those moments of intaking those long stringy bits of deliciousness. And the Tristan stories go on.

EACH LATE FALL LEAVING NORTHERN VIRGINIA IN THE DARK early morning hours, Margaret and Jill arrive in the late after-noon to "sunny and 82" Florida. When everyone else in our area is winding down to hibernate for winter, Margaret and Jill are going in the opposite direction. Florida is the best launch pad for cruises and while on cruises, Margaret, ever kind and generous, leaves goodies such as donuts and bottled water, candies, and mini flashlights for the room stewards and other crew members as tokens of appreciation. On the cruises to Cuba, Margaret tolerated the island stops along the way. The Royal Caribbean's private island with water toys, water slides, and zip lines is no match for the pleasure of the company of the Cuban people.

More like family and dearly loved are Florida friends now over forty-five years, Tony and Florence, and Thomasina and Denny. Thomasina and Denny drive down from Canada for winters and are agreeable to taking care of Tristan when Margaret and Jill go on cruises. More so, Tristan is agreeable to leaving Jill. Their Daytona Shores condominium, high-rise and beach-front, is delightful. Many great friends, a beautiful view of the water, puzzles and books create the perfect winter retreat.

Their Ocean City townhouse provides the perfect summer retreat. The neighbors in Ocean City warm Margaret and Jill's days with friendship and stories, as well. One evening, the mail carrier who lives on their street left his expensive and important work shoes just outside his front door. By morning, one shoe was missing. The following morning, the other shoe was missing. His security camera provided the culprit, the neighborhood fox who turned towards the camera with shoe in mouth as if to say, "I've now taken the other one."

Ocean City provides their summers with a bayside view of the wetlands and waterways. Always in view are tall grasses swept by the wind, sunsets in deep tones, and majestic birds gracefully landing or striding by. Egrets, herons, and willets offer vivid color contrasts. Tristan loves to sit on his window perch and watch all the birds fly in and out of the marsh. Margaret calls the geese that often "sail in,"

"The Armada." The Shore that begins above Ocean City, Maryland and reaches down nearly to Norfolk, Virginia holds beauty Margaret has experienced her whole life.

Everywhere, the joys of Margaret and Jill's friendships abound and could never be matched. They purposefully do not name most of their many friends not to inadvertently omit anyone. "You know who you are and you know the joys of our friendships which could never be matched. We love and appreciate you more than you will ever know."

Good times with friends on the shores of Maryland in summer, the beaches of Florida in winter, and in their neighborhood in suburban Northern Virginia, Margaret and Jill remain eternally grateful.

6

A PEN IS ABOUT PERSPECTIVE

Through the course of writing Margaret's story, I had the good fortune of mentioning "Layton Hall" to my cousin by marriage, Ron in Memphis. Ron has been a genealogy hobbyist from far before he retired and he carved out time to do a little research for us. "Layton" is the last name of a Captain Charles Grimes Layton born in 1782, died in 1856 in Essex County, Virginia which happens to be in the northern end of Tidewater, Virginia, a stretch but no further from where Margaret Savage grew up.

Captain Layton's great granddaughter, Belle Layton Wyatt Willard grew up in the Willard home called "Layton Hall" which sat atop a hill not far from our elementary school. This fine home is in Margaret's memory as she visited there though it was taken down and is not in my memory, or Jill's.

Belle Willard died in 1954. When we were growing up, a school center named "Belle Willard" remained. Now the "Joseph Willard Health Center" named after her father is located on Layton Hall Drive, "Hall" being defined as "a large country house," not anyone's last name as I thought when this writing endeavor began. Layton Hall is also an apartment development, just behind the Joseph Willard Health Center, where Margaret and her father once lived.

The Willard Hotel on Pennsylvania Avenue in Washington, D.C. of the Willard family of Layton Hall in Fairfax is known today for its grand beauty and historic luxury. The Willard family actually sold their share in 1946. Two elementary schools in our city recently merged into one, Layton Hall Elementary School now renovated and renamed Daniels Run Elementary School after the creek behind our school. I still drive by and see that unmistakable 1950's style, still think of Miss Savage, and am grateful we now share her story.

I asked her if she would want Ron to poke around in her family history. The Savage family has a deep history on the Eastern Shore as anyone from there knows. My own college roommate told me so. She grew up in Belle Haven on the Eastern Shore, no relation to Belle Willard. When I went to visit Joanne's home during college, I thought Belle Haven was Joanne's Georgian home and the Presbyterian church just across their country road. Belle Haven, in fact, is a small, quaint town and as mentioned earlier, where Margaret Anne Savage's parents lived when they were still married.

Margaret is the person she is, in so many ways, from growing up running about, experiencing this charming place I unknowingly happened to visit ten years after being in her class. Being a joyful person in the present, Margaret knows where she came from and feels no need to look back at her family history.

Margaret tells me, always maintain the child within. From when she was little, she always allowed the child within her to break out, as did her Mama, Papa, and her mother, Dolly, allow the child within her to break out. They allowed her the freedom to explore her world, to create and imagine, to make discoveries and gain independence, understanding and empathy. Margaret never would hurt anyone. She has always looked at life through other people's eyes and wanted others to feel good.

Volcano models were not made alone at home, she told me during one of our visits. The fun was in bringing everything to school, allowing the child within to break out making volcano models with everyone in class. She taught us by example to maintain the child within.

I will not forget how surprised I was approaching Margaret about writing her story and discovering how much she so vividly remembers. She asked me, in turn, to surprise her with the title. Margaret never forgot her childhood. I never forgot being a child in her class. She has never forgotten the child within and taught us never to forget the child within. Our title became, "The Never Forgotten Child, the Story of our Teacher, Margaret Anne Savage."

NO ONE LIKES TO SAY GOODBYE AT THE END OF A GOOD STORY and this is a hard one for me. When I delivered to Margaret and Jill a hard copy of the final draft still needing review and corrections, I also brought a red pen. I had combed through the story myself with that red pen clearly marking up necessary fixes before going to print. Margaret looked at me and said she had never used a red pen. I almost did not bring it, hesitated as I picked up the fresh-off-the-printer, thick 8 1/2 x11 stack of story. A pen to Margaret is about perspective and she once wrote in our correspondences that her pen sometimes loses perspective. I am thinking now that red ink represents a loss of perspective, the tarnishing of one's ability to learn, something Margaret would not engage in.

I've read this over and again in putting together

Margaret's words with her help with my help. We gained our perspective together and invited you in. I love her now as I loved her in sixth grade. There will always be more to say about her life than said. She enjoys fried chicken wings and fajitas, mashed potatoes and the color blue. She does not like liver or eggs, guns and violence, or snakes. She will watch horse racing on television and she will not watch horror movies. Her favorites are British comedies and murder mysteries, The Durrells in Corfu, Fawlty Towers, and Black Adder, Downton Abbey, and Monty Python.

Her favorite books, anything by Jeffrey Archer and over time, still "Don Quixote," "The Hunchback of Notre Dame," and "Les Miserable" and that's just a start. I can't keep up though now I will try for Margaret Savage brings out the best in us. She has read the entire Bible three times and loves the verse about love, 1 Corinthians 13:13 "And now these three remain: faith, hope, and love. But the greatest of these is love." She loves animals and kind people and doesn't like when people lie or pretend to be religious when they are not and then do rotten things. At her age now, she can say these things because they are true but then, she has always been true to herself.

The Savage side of her family are not worriers and that's how I see Margaret. Jill who knows her best says she is a worrier like the dog on television who worries his bone is not safe and continues to dig it up to hide it elsewhere. Maybe that's from the Kilmon side of the family as farmers do have to worry, too much rain or too little rain, crop yield, and on. I feel comfortable and life's worries seem to lift settling down in their home today enjoying a fresh made Kentucky mule cocktail in that lovely hammered copper mug.

How is Miss Savage? She is well. Jill is right there with her, healthy, harmonious, humorous, and happiness. Margaret makes a list each evening for the day to come and wakes to accomplish what is set before her. I won't forget how at home she was in our classroom back in 1969 because she is at home with herself, warm and accepting to this day in 2019.

She tells me as a teacher, she wanted her students to have all the good she found growing up and to be able to avoid tribulation. She wanted them to be able to laugh at themselves, to respect themselves, and to respect others, all religions and cultures. She wanted her students to be kind and to love, to love animals and art and music, and to be true to themselves.

Her childhood reveals a young girl named Moggy who was loved and loved back, who understood early on what was important, young Moggy who was Margaret Anne, "just call me Margaret or whatever you wish." I call her Joyful. She brought love and laughter and happiness, her fun and her antics into our classroom. Children need smiles and she gave them each day. She gave her students permission to be their authentic selves as she was her authentic self, allowing the child within to break out, the child never forgotten. As her own childhood will always be remembered and never forgotten, Miss Savage will always be remembered and never forgotten.

HER CHILDHOOD REVEALS
THE YOUNG GIRL SHE WAS,
THE TEACHER SHE BECAME.

-

MOGGY WHO WAS MARGARET ANNE,
"JUST CALL ME MARGARET OR WHATEVER YOU WISH."

-

FOREVER FUN, FULL OF ANTICS,
LOVE AND LAUGHTER.
TRUE TO HERSELF.

-

AS HER CHILDHOOD,
ALWAYS REMEMBERED, NEVER FORGOTTEN,

-

JOYFUL
MISS SAVAGE.

STILL NOT TIED TO A MAST

Silver Beach, Eastern Shore of Virginia, 1940's

Annie Rebecca Kilmon, Mama, before she married Papa

John Revell Kilmon, Papa with Mama

Margaret with her mother

Mama and Papa's farmhouse Margaret grew up in

Margaret's mother, Dolly, beautiful like a movie star

Margaret and Dolly

With Baby Bear before Baby Lamb came along

Rootin' Tootin' Cowgirl

Papa, Margaret, Cousin Bob and his father, Uncle Buck

Margaret's father, Jim Savage

With Cousin Nancy from the Savage side of the family

College roommate, Nitti, with Cousin Bob

Don, Bob, Margaret, and Nitti

With Ronnie Nelson, often barefoot

Margaret on her speed boat

With Sabra, the Belgian Alsatian dog, in the 1953 MG TD

Tristan in-between Jill and Margaret

Margaret hanging from the ceiling

Treasures always found metal detecting

In Daytona Shores, Florida claiming territory

Jill and Margaret with her brother, JK, James Kendal

Marghieth and JK

Mrs. Nottingham, age 100

MAya Savage reigns supreme

Jill, double-fisted

JAN PRICE

Dennis and Thomasina

In a 1950's American-made car, painted purple in Cuba

In a carriage in Cuba

Thoughtful to the cruise concierge

Always kind, always appreciative

Still not tied to a mast

Cousin Dennis from the Savage side of the family

*With Cousin Linda from Papa's side of the family, her
daughter, Garibaldis and Gari's husband, Steve*

And then a giant bird swooped in